I HATE SCHOOL

Also by Cynthia Ulrich Tobias

The Way They Learn
Every Child Can Succeed
The Way We Work
Bringing Out the Best in Your Child
Do You Know What I Like about You?
You Can't Make Me (But I Can Be Persuaded)
Redefining the Strong-Willed Woman

HOW

TO HELP

YOUR CHILD

LOVE

LEARNING

I HATE SCHOOL

CYNTHIA ULRICH TOBIAS

GRAND RAPIDS, MICHIGAN 49530 USA

We want to hear from you. Please send your comments about this book to us in care of zreview@zondervan.com. Thank you.

ZONDERVAN™

I Hate School

Requests for information should be addressed to:

Zondervan, *Grand Rapids, Michigan 49530*

Library of Congress Cataloging-in-Publication Data

Tobias, Cynthis Ulrich, 1953–
I hate school : how to help your child love learning / Cynthia Ulrich Tobias.
p. cm.
Includes bibliographical references.
ISBN 0-310-24577-X
1. Motivation in education. 2. Education—Parent participation.
I. Title.
LB1065 .T59 2004
370.15'4—dc22

2003023100

Published in association with the literary agency of Alive Communications, Inc., 7680 Goddard Street, Suite 200, Colorado Springs, CO 80920.

Interior design by Michelle Espinoza

Printed in the United States of America

---

04 05 06 07 08 09 10 /❖ DC/ 10 9 8 7 6 5 4 3 2 1

To my sons, Michael and Robert Tobias,
who demonstrate daily that learning is not a rote
exercise to give uniform structure and discipline to
young minds. Mike and Rob are shining examples of
how learning is a living, growing world of discovery,
full of opportunities to create confident capable
individuals who can change the world!

CONTENTS

Part 4: Changing the School, Not Your Child

1 School: The Shoe That Needs to Fit

Why do so many children now struggle to learn, especially when it comes to particulars like detailed directions, rules of grammar and spelling, and math facts? We need better explanations than naming and blaming our children for having deficiencies. Could it be that to a degree, our mind-set and educational format have outlived their usefulness? Every day we expect children to adapt to our way of thinking. Is it time to update our thinking and be more open to the potential of theirs?

—Lucy Jo Palladino, *The Edison Trait*

I was standing outside the Chip 'n Dale play area at Disneyland, watching as the children inside screamed with delight, enthusiastically jumping and racing around. One father who stood beside me seemed agitated, and kept calling out to his son, trying to get him to calm down. After several attempts to get his son's attention, the dad turned to me with an exasperated look on his face and said, "See what we get when he's off his Ritalin?"

I must have looked more surprised than supportive, because he quickly moved away so he could retrieve his son. I wanted to remind this frustrated father that this was *Disneyland*—a place where kids are *expected* to be excited and energetic.

The sad truth is that more and more children are expected to be calm and obedient regardless of the circumstances, and the diagnosis of and medication for learning and attention deficit disorders is becoming more and more popular, even for very young children. Recent studies have shown that seven to ten percent or more of America's school-age children are being prescribed stimulant drugs to control their behavior, and the actual figures may be higher. The percentage of boys being drugged is disproportionately large and probably reaches or exceeds fifteen to twenty percent. Some drug advocates believe that eight million of America's children should be taking some kind of psychiatric medication. For 1997 the DEA authorized 13,824 kilograms [of Ritalin], an increase of more than seven hundred percent since 1990.[1]

When my first book, *The Way They Learn,* was released over ten years ago, it was received with great enthusiasm. Parents and teachers all over the world embraced the idea of discovering each child's individual learning strengths and focusing on strategies for bringing out the best in each student. These learning styles include traits that can be very inconvenient for a standard classroom or an intolerant adult. Many children need movement and physical activity to be at their best; others need to verbalize their thoughts and talk their way through tasks. Virtually all children need to experiment with the discovery process of learning—and that can be messy. Strong-willed children challenge authority to establish boundaries and parameters, and they seldom just meekly obey. As they grow through the different stages of their lives, children can be noisy and irritating and full of questions. They can annoy and frustrate adults who prefer to keep situations calm and stay in control. Anyone who is involved in working with children knows these statements are true. Unfortunately, many adults who do work with children seem to have forgotten that we cannot expect to effectively teach and nurture the younger generation if our focus is on keeping circumstances and outcomes convenient for us. Especially when it comes to education, we are not the customer—the *student* is the customer. And yet, in my almost two decades of working with parents and educators, there is a growing concern that instead of truly identifying and meeting the needs of students, society in general and the educational system specifically is choosing to medicate them into the kind of conformity that is most convenient for the adults who teach them.

There are children who have very legitimate physiological and neurological disabilities. But for every one of those children, what if we're putting ten other normal but inconvenient children in the same group? The children who truly need the professional attention have their treatment diluted by those who suffer the fate of being misdiagnosed and categorized as learning disabled or behavior problems.

It becomes even more alarming when you consider the fact that once students graduate from their K–12 education, they usually get hired for the very things they got in *trouble* for when they were in school. Human resources managers have a few very consistent requirements, regardless of the type of position they are filling. The best applicants should have good social interaction, independent thinking skills, and a high energy level, among other things. If you think about it, we not only don't foster those traits in school, we often actively *discourage* them. If we are spending a great deal of time diagnosing and medicating students so they can conform to a classroom situation that becomes virtually irrelevant after it's over, what's the point?

I am *not* advocating a permissive and lenient education system. I do not believe we should lower academic standards or compromise when it comes to good behavior. I am totally committed to accountability. But what is it we are trying to measure? Have we actually asked and answered this important question: *What's the point?* If we simply demand that students do what we tell them and work hard because they have to, how many will want to keep on learning when the required formal education is complete?

When I take my children to the shoe store and the shoes don't fit, I can't change their feet. They *do* need to wear shoes, though, so we keep shopping until we find the shoes that fit their feet. What worries me about education is that from the very beginning we have offered very few styles of "shoes." When a child's foot won't fit the shoe we offer, we insist that the *foot* be changed. But what happens when you force a child's foot into uncomfortable and ill-fitting shoes and make him walk around in them? As soon as he possibly can, he takes the shoes off, vowing never to put them on again. I can't count the times I have had mature and capable adults come up to me when I was doing a corporate workshop and say, "Look, I know I'm stuck in a boring, dead-end job—but I'd rather stay here *forever* than go back to school." They remember quite well what those shoes felt like, and they have no desire to put them on again. Companies spend millions on training programs and many even provide financial incentives for employees to get college degrees. And yet so many adults have vivid memories of being in a classroom, feeling stupid or overwhelmed with tasks of concentration and memory they are ill-equipped to undertake. If the formal process of education is mostly a dreaded chore to be done or is tantamount to a prison sentence to be served, why should we be surprised when each successive generation becomes less and less interested in applying themselves to the task of learning? How can we justify making children suffer a boring and sometimes even painful educational experience if the end result is that they never want to learn again?

We *do* need educational reform, but most of all we need to remember *who* we are trying to educate. The students should be our first priority—each child should be considered an important and valuable customer who can potentially change the world for the better. We should keep our standards high, our academic goals clear, and our code of ethics strong. The *point* is, we need to teach kids to think, not just feed them facts to think *about*. That means we'll need to pay attention to the individual learning strengths and preferences of each student. It means we can't just put them through classrooms full of uniform fixtures and standard requirements and expect them to all come out equally proficient. Most importantly, it means we have to stop focusing on how the schools can meet the needs of teachers, administrators, and custodians and start looking for ways the schools can serve the true customer—the student. We need to stay vigilant and keep our eyes on the goals—and we need to make sure we know what the goals *are,* not just dictate methods for getting students to do what we want.

Education *is* currently in trouble, but I believe that until we clearly define where we are going, no amount of legislation and funding will help us get there. In business, we don't take a product that is inferior and seek to improve it by opening more factories, increasing employees, and instituting longer working hours without first finding out why the product is inferior in the first place. We have missed the point. I believe "Outcome-Based Education" has turned out to be a convoluted concept that no one can define and that simply can't be salvaged. But education *needs* to be about legitimate outcomes and accountability. I'd like to call it "What's the Point?" education. I'd love to see educators and parents and businesspeople sitting down together and asking questions like, "What do these kids need to know?" "What should each student be able to do when we're through teaching them this?" "What are we trying to measure?"

For me, the least appealing aspect of bowling has always been the fact that you have to wear someone else's shoes. The sizes that are offered are standard, and if your foot doesn't conform to any of them, you just have to adjust and choose the closest fit. You put on the exact same pair of shoes that dozens of strangers have worn. You could, of course, choose to bring your *own* shoes, but they must be a special kind approved by the bowling alley, and the price tag is a bit steep for someone who isn't all that serious about the game. It didn't take me long to avoid going to bowling alleys completely. Unfortunately, many children feel the very same way about school. For many students, school was such a poor fit that it's simply not the best measure of their intelligence or abilities. For some parents, private schools are an option, and for others homeschooling is a possibility—but almost any alternative costs more, and some parents will never be able to afford the price tag. Eventually, many students avoid learning altogether.

When Shaquille O'Neill entered the basketball scene a few years ago, he needed a *size 20* shoe. None of us had even imagined an athletic shoe size that went that high. It's hard to imagine that we would say to him, "I'm sorry, son, but this is the biggest athletic shoe we make—you'll just have to squeeze your foot in and do the best you can." We didn't even think twice about custom-making a shoe that fit those talented feet, and "Shaq" made a tremendous impact on the world of professional basketball. Are our children any less precious or important?

It doesn't mean we have to give every child a custom education. Not every pair of shoes in our closet fits equally comfortably. We have certain pairs of shoes we wear for short periods of time for specific occasions. But most of us have shoes in our closet that have one thing in common: they all come in the size that fits our foot. If we can begin to recognize and appreciate natural individual learning style strengths in our students, I am convinced we can begin to broaden the variety of shoes in every educational closet. This book will offer practical and immediately useful strategies for finding shoes that fit the feet of the child instead of insisting that those precious and uniquely designed feet must always adjust to the shoes that are provided.

There are so many reasons students could be struggling in school that have nothing to do with innate intelligence, natural abilities, or even how hard they try. So often, it's not the foot that's the problem—it's the shoe. Keep an open mind as you continue reading, and you may discover some pretty amazing ways to measure feet and shop for all kinds of shoes!

Step on in . . .

PART 1

THE PHYSICAL ENVIRONMENT

2 Sometimes School Happens at the Wrong Time of Day

Parents should not despair; some children with a sleep-arousal imbalance may turn out to be the next generation of night people. They may compose cello sonatas at 2:00 a.m., work the night shift at the BMW plant, or host an all-night radio rock show. Regrettably, during childhood, tomorrow's night owls are condemned to attend school with all the day kids. We don't yet offer night schools for night children.

—Mel Levine, M.D., *A Mind at a Time*

Jason, this is your *final warning*! Get up *right now!* You're going to miss the school bus—and I'm not going to drive you to school again."

Cathy is pretty much at the end of her rope with her sixteen-year-old son. Jason is such a great kid, she tells me. He's class president this year and is in at least two honors classes. *"But I can't get him up in the morning!"* she says through clenched teeth. She's been up since 6 A.M. and the coffee is on, breakfast is ready, and two loads of wash are almost done.

"If Jason would go to *sleep* before midnight every night, we wouldn't have this early morning battle," she points out. "But I can't even get him *started* on his homework before 10 P.M. and I'm already half asleep. He would happily stay up all night."

Roberta's mom has the opposite problem. Her fourth-grade daughter gets up earlier than anyone else in the house. By the time Mom is up, Roberta is dressed and reading her newest book on the couch. Mom still feels sleepy when she drops her off at the private Christian school she attends. "But," her mom laments, "it's like pulling teeth to get Roberta to do her homework when she comes in from school."

By 3:30 in the afternoon, Roberta's mom is fully alert and actively dealing with her day. Her part-time job starts at 10 A.M. and ends at 3 P.M. so she can work her schedule around her family. When she gets home she can't understand why everyone else isn't as ready as she is to accomplish the tasks that need to be done.

Most of us are at our best at certain times of day, and at our worst at others. We truly do have an "inner clock" that sets our energy and concentration levels higher during some hours than others. Jason is a night owl, and he usually can't quite fully wake up before 10 A.M. Morning is his mom's best time of day, and she can't understand why it's so difficult for Jason to just discipline himself to go to bed early enough to be more alert in the morning. He and his mom often argue over the most minor issues in the morning, and she frequently feels guilty when he leaves so grouchy. His very first class is math—not his best subject—and he already has at least two strikes against him. No matter how hard he tries to concentrate, there are "cobwebs" in his head. His frustration level is already high when he has to leave the house so early; now it's compounded by the feeling of failure in a class where he knows he has to get a passing grade.

Roberta is bright and sharp in the early morning hours, but she struggles to even stay awake during her afternoon subjects. When the final bell rings and she gets to come home, her mom wants her to get right to the homework that needs to be done. For a morning person, the worst time of day to do anything that takes mental effort and concentration is the late afternoon, and Roberta often sits in frustration at the table with her books in front of her. Her mom has to remind her several times to get busy and finish before dinner, but usually the "reminders" turn into arguments, and by evening both Roberta and her mom are out of sorts and irritated with each other.

For as long as anyone can remember, traditional school has started early in the morning and ended in the midafternoon. Parents, teachers, administrators—everyone must adapt to that schedule. For some, starting early is ideal; for many, it's daily punishment for staying up too late the night before. The fact is, many industries rely on shift work. It's not like the whole country puts in the same workday. I want the police officer working the graveyard shift to be a night person. I'd like the swing-shift factory worker who builds the engine for my car to be very alert at 4:30 in the afternoon.

But how does education help identify and foster the strengths of those who are not at their best during the typical school day? If one of the objectives of a good education is to prepare our children for the work world, how can we so completely overlook this aspect of it? Jason and Roberta are both very good students. If the challenge is this great for kids who are high achievers in spite of doing their hardest tasks at their worst time of day, what must it be like for the less motivated ones?

You might be surprised to know that many teachers struggle with the very same time-of-day issues as their students. Around the country, I often ask groups of teachers and administrators how many of them would like school to start at 6 A.M. and be done at noon. About 50 percent of the hands usually go up. How many would prefer to start school at noon and end at 6 P.M.? The other 50 percent invariably volunteer. When I pose these same questions to students, I get almost identical results.

IN THEIR OWN WORDS

I think I'd learn better at school if I got more sleep in the morning—I am getting F's and D's, and if I got more sleep I would get A's for sure.

—Thomas, eighth grade

Most schools will tell you it would be a nightmare to try and adapt the master schedule so that all students could take their hardest classes at their best time of day. Realistically, that's probably not going to happen anytime soon. But there could be much more flexibility than we currently offer. It doesn't take too many minds getting together to figure out some creative alternatives to a "one-size-fits-all" schedule—especially if they are committed to the idea that students are the primary customers.

In her book *Learning Styles: A Quiet Revolution,* Rita Dunn tells about Sacred Heart Seminary, a private school in New York that decided to adapt their schedule to the students instead of the other way around.

> Sacred Heart, therefore, adopted an eight-day time frame that alternates classes in a cycle, enabling each youngster to attend basic courses at their best time of day at least some of the time. . . . Every attempt is made to accommodate students' preferred time of day through flexible scheduling and rotation of classes by cycle so that all courses are taught at some time during students' peak energy periods.[2]

There are many schools across the country that have the determination and commitment to design a schedule that helps students be more productive. There doesn't have to be drastic reform all at once in order to see improvement. Sacred Heart decided at the very least, when it comes to taking critical standardized achievement or placement tests, we should be aware of when a student is at his or her best:

> For example, eighth graders are allowed to select their preferred time of day for taking the standardized achievement test. . . . In 1986–87, the seminary administered the Iowa Test of Basic Skills to all its students in two different time frames—early morning and afternoon. Morning preferents took the test then, and afternoon high-energy youngsters attended the afternoon administration.[3]

I don't think there's much argument that most schools schedule virtually every test they give at a time that is most convenient for administration and measurement, not for the preferences of the students. For some administrations, it would seem like an admission of weakness to let students dictate the time and place for standardized tests. After all, who's in charge here? But *what's the point?* If the point is to find out what the students have learned, doesn't it make sense to test them at a time when they have the best chance to recall the information?

During the course of their education, students need to know what works best for them when it comes to learning. At the very least, we need to teach them to be aware of the obstacles that may keep them from being at their best so that when they *do* have a choice they can make the right one. As adults, we have certainly had to learn to accommodate the schedules of others. But most of us do our best to avoid doing difficult tasks at our lowest energy point in the day. Shouldn't we at least be teaching our children to recognize when they're at their best so they can consciously adapt also?

IN THEIR OWN WORDS

Having shorter, more intense school days would be awesome. Like an 8 A.M.–noon school day that was packed with learning, and then go home and do work. Today, for example, it took almost thirty minutes to start class. We could have been doing other things.

—Angela, twelfth grade

Schools who have adopted a more flexible schedule for students are often surprised at the positive results. Although teachers and administrators feared that they would be giving too much control to the students, the students actually were better behaved and disciplined when they had the freedom to make individual choices. Take, for example, a high school in rural Wyoming:

> The school has adopted alternative schedules, permitting the core curriculum to be taught in the morning one week and in the afternoon the next, to avoid favoring only one chronobiological preference. The average number of absences per year decreased significantly after learning styles instruction was initiated, and overall achievement gains reflect that 73 percent of students are now on grade level or higher as measured by the Stanford Achievement Test.[4]

Unfortunately, for the most part the only schools that are offering any flexibility in schedule are the alternative schools. Evening and night classes are popular with many students who would otherwise have dropped out of school entirely, even though students in traditional school may benefit from having the option too. I know it would take a lot of effort initially to redesign a schedule that is most effective for the greatest number of students. It would certainly take a different mind-set—we would have to start thinking about being student-centered, and we're not really accustomed to that idea. It's not that educators don't care about students—by far, the majority of them do. It's just that for generations we have been conditioned to force the student to adjust to the system, regardless of how poorly the system may fit. It's much easier to simply let the system keep on the way it is and spend more money and effort figuring out ways to get the students to conform whether they like it or not.

What Can We Do in the Meantime?

Since school starts pretty early, the cause of a lot of morning battles can be traced to the fact that your night owl child simply doesn't *function* well before 10 A.M. That doesn't mean you have to find a school that starts later, but you *can* help your child cope with the cobwebs that fill his or her head in the early morning hours. Use the evening hours to do as much preparation for morning as possible. Find the school books, the backpack, the necessary slips of paper, and set them all out by the door. Make all the morning decisions you can before bedtime—what will you have for breakfast? What time will you leave for school? What clothes will you wear? Help your child figure out how late he can sleep and still make it out the door on time. (This may take a little trial and error!) Maybe *you're* the one who doesn't do mornings—stop driving yourself crazy with last-minute arguments and try to simply focus on what has to be done.

IN THEIR OWN WORDS

What if school started a period earlier and ended a period later, and students got to pick the periods to come (i.e., 2–7 or 1–6)?

—Mike, twelfth grade

A lot of kids don't seem to do mornings well, but there are at least as many who do mornings *best*. The best time for them is the fresh dawning of a new day, and they wake with clear heads and light hearts. These same morning kids, though, fade fast after lunch, and the afternoon hours are almost torturous. They've had a tough time staying awake and concentrating in their afternoon classes, and as soon as they get home they dread sitting down at that desk again and applying themselves to more study before dinner. They're tired and cranky, and there will be arguments. Try letting them unwind when they get home—let them relax before dinner and get the cobwebs out of their brains. See if doing their homework in the *morning* might work better. Getting up an hour earlier may be a lot easier than arguing unproductively for two hours before dinner.

The Homeschool Advantage

If you are homeschooling, you automatically have the advantage of a more flexible schedule. And yet, for a variety of reasons, homeschool parents frequently want to enforce a schedule consistent with a traditional school day. For many children, that works very well, but if you have more than one child, you'll probably run into the same time-of-day issues that happen in a formal classroom. Of course, it would be much easier on you if everyone would do their schoolwork at the same time. But encouraging your children to find and use their most productive time of day can go a long way in helping them become more effective learners.

Challenge the kids themselves to experiment with various times of day or night to see what seems to work best when they have to concentrate on a difficult task. Help them appreciate what works for each other, encouraging them to look for ways of increasing productivity without spending unnecessary time and effort. Point out that sometimes everyone has to do difficult things at less-than-favorite times of day, but that understanding and awareness is at least half the battle. If you know going in that it's going to be more frustrating to you, it often turns out not to be so bad after all!

STRETCHING THE SHOE

Some Practical and Immediate Adaptations

- Whenever possible, help your children schedule their hardest tasks for their best and most alert times of day.
- Help each child plan to do homework or test review at his or her own best time for concentration; develop ways your child can stay alert when it's going to be difficult—a cold drink, a snack, whatever seems to wake the senses up the best.
- Add some of your own ideas:

____

____

____

CHANGING THE SHOE

Some Ideal Solutions

- Redesign the times we schedule school, offering more alternatives that include evening and night classes as well as early morning sessions.
- Try a four-day school week, with a more intense schedule during the day, but an extra day on the weekend for work or reflection.

- Find a way to let students take the standardized tests at the time of day when they are most alert.
- Add some of your own ideas:

____

____

____

TRY IT OUT

Try charting your own hours of peak energy and alertness. Then have other family members or coworkers chart theirs. Compare and discuss the charts—it can provide some very interesting conversations!

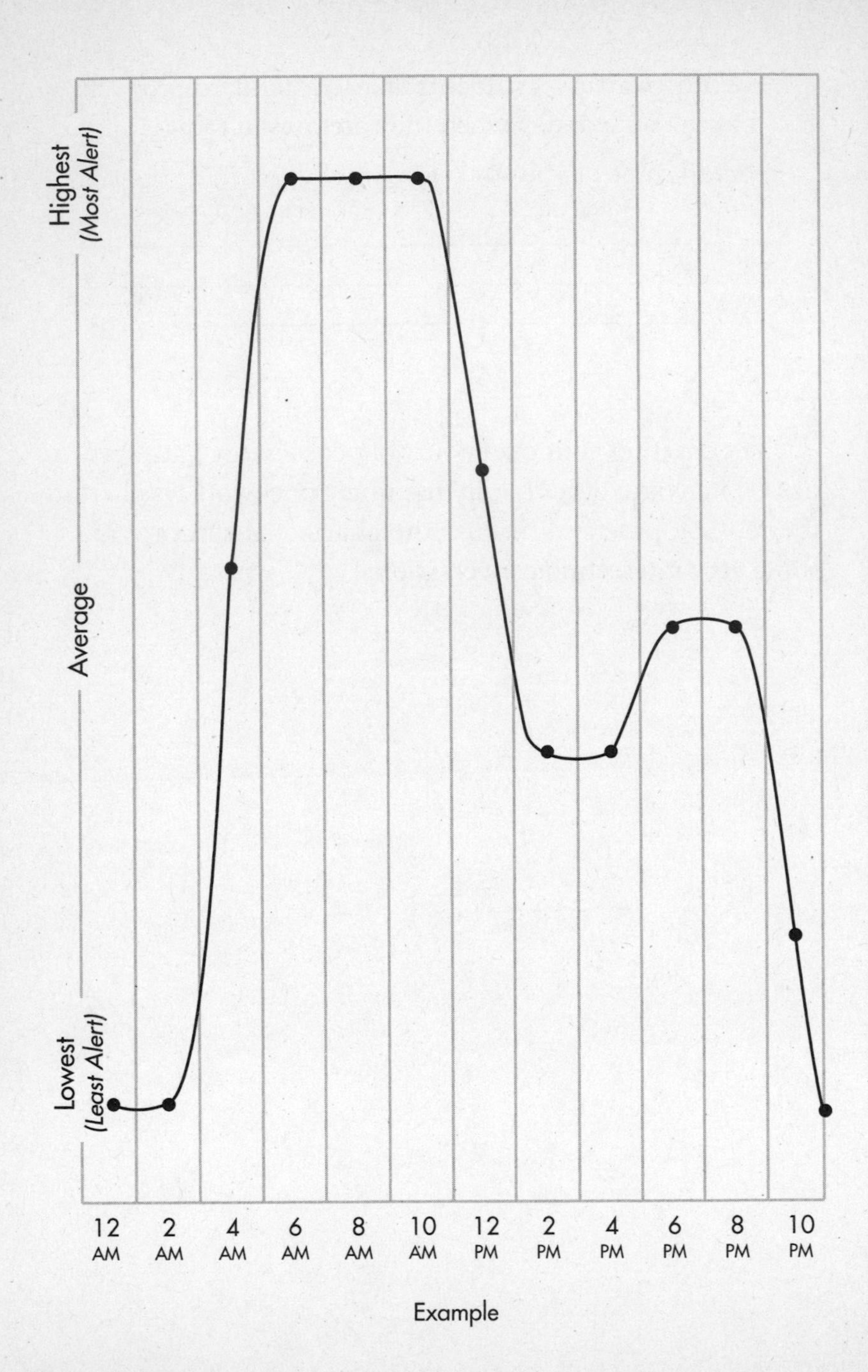
Highest
(Most Alert)
Average
Lowest
(Least Alert)
12 AM
2 AM
4 AM
6 AM
8 AM
10 AM
12 PM
2 PM
4 PM
6 PM
8 PM
10 PM
Example

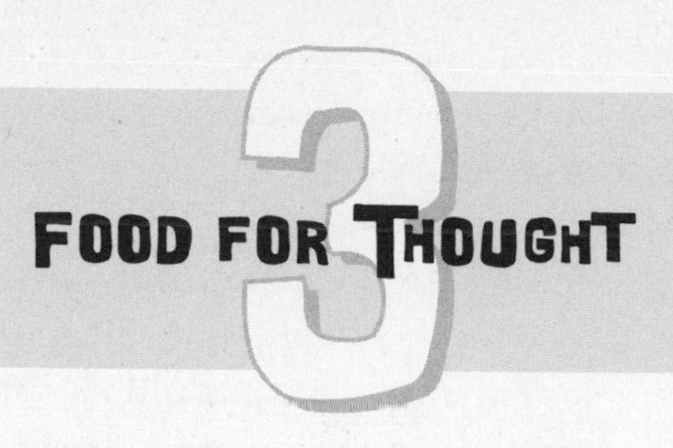

3 Food for Thought

Learning occurs best when learners enjoy the process. . . . Learning is effective when it creates learner appetite for more learning and an insatiable desire to share the learning with others.

—Thom and Joni Schultz, *The Dirt on Learning*

The sign read: NO FOOD OR DRINK ALLOWED IN THE AUDITORIUM. Oh, no—I know I'm in trouble already! Even though I am a mature adult, this sign almost always signals an obstacle for my attention span. I've always listened and paid better attention if I have a cup of coffee or bottle of water in my hand. It doesn't have to be much—but if I can't have *anything*, my distraction level automatically increases. I usually end up sitting there wishing I had sneaked at least a piece of hard candy into my purse, and before I know it I miss the first few minutes of the presentation. When I finally force myself to focus, it doesn't take long before I start wondering when the break will be and my mind starts to wander again. You'd think I could get over the need to have something to eat or drink—after all, there's a time and place for everything, right? But over the years, I've discovered it's easier to just keep an emergency stash of cinnamon candy or mints wherever I go just in case I need them.

Most school classrooms won't allow food or drink, and yet it's very common to see something on the *teacher's* desk—a bottle of water, a handful of M&Ms, a cup of coffee. It's also common to see several children sitting at their desks biting their nails or chewing on the end of a pencil. It's not always just a nervous habit; often it's a substitution for something to nibble on or to drink. There are many good reasons for insisting that students not have refreshments in the classroom—it can be messy, unhealthy, distracting, and inconvenient for the teacher and custodial staff. But there's one major reason we *should* consider relaxing the rule a bit: For many students, something as minor as having a quick snack can make the difference between listening and tuning out. After all, if you are a student who really needs to eat or drink in order to pay attention and the teacher won't let you eat or drink, what are you thinking about while the teacher is talking? That's right—eating and drinking! So what's the point? If the point is listening and remembering what was taught, and eating or drinking helps you do that, shouldn't we at least give you the chance to prove it?

I'm not advocating unbridled chaos or giving out bags of candy and letting all the students do whatever they want. Accountability must always stay intact, and children should not get away with using their learning style as an excuse. But the issue of needing some kind of intake while learning could prove to be a key factor in helping a lot of kids pay attention in class. It's one of the lines of first defense we can take down before we decide a child has a more serious neurological problem.

When I first discovered the whole concept of learning styles, I was teaching high school English, and I was eager to experiment with different strategies to see if I could help my students improve. I had one class of historically low achievers. No one really expected these kids to get much better than a passing grade; my duty was just to help them squeak by until graduation. I started talking to them about learning styles, and we decided together that we would find as many ways as possible to identify and use our individual learning strengths. When it came to the subject of intake, I approached my principal for permission to conduct an experiment. We had carpeted classrooms and rather controlling and grouchy custodians, so I had to practically sedate my principal to get him to agree to my plan. My proposal was modest, I thought. I would not allow drinks, since the water fountain was right outside the door and a quick drink was easy to obtain. Students could eat in class, but not just anything. There were limitations to what they could bring as snacks: nothing that was eaten noisily, no junk food, nothing that would be greasy or leave a crumby mess, nothing that would distract others sitting nearby. The kids themselves came up with some good suggestions: a granola bar, a handful of peanuts, a couple pieces of red licorice, and so on. If any wrappers or

IN THEIR OWN WORDS

I would have a snack cart in every classroom so if you got hungry before or after lunch you could buy something.

—Danielle, twelfth grade

other trash was left behind, the privilege of eating would be immediately suspended. Oh, and one more, most important thing: They had to *prove* that eating something in class actually helped them listen and pay attention.

I have to admit I was a little worried at first. For three days, it seemed like *everyone* brought something to eat. My principal paced nervously outside the door, and I kept gently reminding my students that their work would have to be the proof that this new privilege was a good idea. By the end of the week, I noticed that only about a fourth of the class was still bringing something to eat. But I also noticed that they were actually looking at me and listening while they were munching. Some of these were students who had always struggled with paying attention in class, and yet something as simple as eating seemed to help them focus on what was being taught. For those who insisted they needed it, I let them eat even while they were taking a test—as long as they could prove their scores were better if they did.

For many of us, whether we are adults or children, being able to eat or drink while learning symbolizes something more than simply meeting a physical need. If you think about it, bringing refreshments to any class or meeting seems to indicate a more relaxed, friendly, informal atmosphere. Certainly there are times when it is necessary to set a formal tone, but if the point is to put students in a place where they feel comfortable enough to learn, having some form of intake can make the difference between dreading a class and actually looking forward to it.

I've always thought it was interesting that at least one adult Sunday school class in almost every church in America offers coffee and donuts before class to entice people to come. Of course, the adults spend a lot of their refreshment time chasing children away from the table. It's pretty rare to find refreshments in children's Sunday school classes, even though they would probably appreciate it even more than the adults do. The churches that have been willing to experiment find that there's no need to offer sugary treats—often just a big bowl of Chex Mix or Cheerios available during class makes a remarkable difference in how many children look forward to coming to class on Sunday morning.

You might be surprised to find out how the simple act of serving food or drink in a classroom setting can put many students at ease and give them the confidence to share and interact with their teacher and classmates. You may also discover that allowing your child to eat or drink while studying at home makes the work seem easier and more pleasant. It seems to be such a small thing—isn't it at least worth a try?

IN THEIR OWN WORDS

I don't think eating in class would be a problem as long as students clean up after themselves and don't disrupt class with it.

—John, high school student

The Homeschool Advantage

Homeschool students usually have many more opportunities to snack on something in between lessons. However, if the parent who is homeschooling does not share the preference for eating and drinking while learning, he or she may not understand a child's insistence on nibbling during a lesson. There are many adults for whom refreshments would actually be more of a distraction than a help, so it's not surprising that they may firmly believe the snack should be a reward for getting an assignment done, not an instructional aid during the process. Also, if there are several children being homeschooled at once, chances are good that some of them won't benefit by the intake that others so depend upon. Again, the most important thing you can do is to discuss the issue openly and encourage your children to experiment with what actually works. Although "home economics" is an outdated term, a little knowledge about nutrition and cooking can be a valuable addition to your children's education. Why not challenge your kids to find the snacks that give the most brain power, then let them prove it!

STRETCHING THE SHOE

Some Practical and Immediate Adaptations

- Get permission from your child's teacher to either bring a bottle of water or to take two or three quick trips to the drinking fountain during class.
- Encourage your child to eat or drink something right before going into the classroom—and keep a quick snack handy for in between classes when necessary.
- Add some of your own ideas:

____

____

____

CHANGING THE SHOE

Some Ideal Solutions

- Have healthy, appealing snacks for all students who want them available throughout the day—make sure everyone knows they are responsible for keeping the area clean in order to keep the privilege.
- Allow students to bring their own snacks, using guidelines you give them (i.e., relatively healthy, not messy, not distracting to others, and so on). Again, if their area is not kept clean, the privilege is lost.
- Add some of your own ideas:

____

____

____

TRY IT OUT

Chart your personal preferences for eating or drinking while you relax, work, or learn. Then encourage others to chart theirs as well, and compare and discuss.

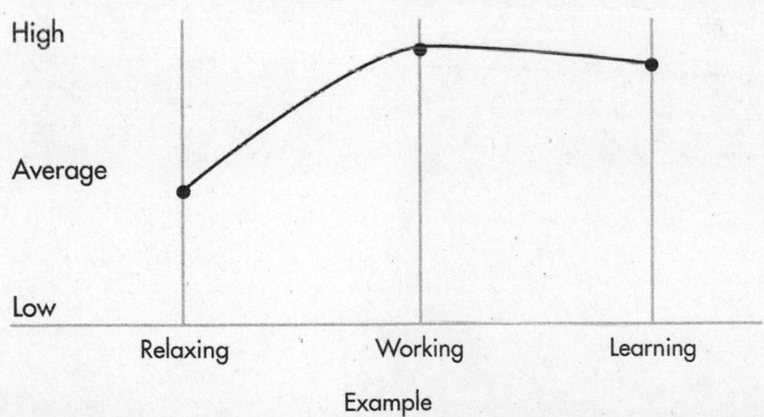

Example

4 LET THERE BE LIGHT

If our focus is merely on teachers and teaching, we'll produce little fruit. But if our focus shifts to the learner, it'll change everything we do.

—Thom and Joni Shultz, *The Dirt on Learning*

It was the first day of class for eighteen preschoolers—four- and five-year-olds—and their teachers were trying an informal experiment. There were several play areas throughout the room, all with similar or identical toys. The only real difference was the lighting. Part of the room was flooded with sunlight, brought through a large window. Another area was much darker, lit only with a table lamp. Another corner was much brighter, lit by two halogen floor lamps. At least one corner had the traditional fluorescent lighting, and the last corner had almost no light at all, illuminated only by the residual effects of the lighting in the rest of the room.

Observers stood by as the children arrived. How much difference would the light make? Would it overcome other variables such as favorite playmates? It didn't take long to find out. That morning, and over the course of the next two weeks, these preschoolers demonstrated a surprising consistency when it came to playing in the area of the room that seemed most comfortable to them. Some children seemed perfectly content to play in the almost-dark corner. Others repeatedly went to the sun-drenched triangle. Still others seemed to be relatively unaffected by light at all, and played happily in several different areas.

IN THEIR OWN WORDS

I find that I learn a lot better in rooms with windows and with the blinds open than learning in a closed classroom with no windows.

—Tammy, twelfth grade

Considering the age of the children, the teachers had to admit there's no way they could have been coached ahead of time. Even though there are obviously several variables, the teachers kept track most of the year and concluded that several of the children had very consistent preferences when it came to the light where they worked or played.

Growing up, most of us have heard our parents say, "Turn up the light—you're going to ruin your eyes reading in light like that!" Now it turns out that each individual only needs enough light so they are not straining their eyes to see. That means that some kids can read comfortably with practically no light at all. Others need as much bright light as possible, and still others are somewhere in between. So maybe it's not just because it saves on the power bill that someone goes through the house turning off or down all the lights that another family member just turned on.

In offices, we adults often make all sorts of adjustments to make sure we work in light that's appropriate for our needs. Some turn off the overhead lights and bring lamps; others make sure they have a source of natural light somewhere in the office. But students have little or no control over their lighting at school. Virtually every school building in America uses fluorescent bulbs as the primary source of light. Several reports have indicated that certain fluorescent bulbs can actually be at the very least distracting for many students, and at worst, physically harmful. Fluorescent lights have been known to trigger seizures, migraine headaches, and learning difficulties.

Obviously not everyone is sensitive to lighting issues, but for some it can be a contributing factor to a lack of concentration. It may not be an issue for your child, but what if it is? What if, by simply adjusting the light, you could improve your child's focus and attention?

It's not always easy to make adjustments in a traditional classroom, but as a teacher I looked for creative ways to make even minor adjustments. I turned off one bank of fluorescent lights, and I put colored tissue paper in another fixture to diffuse the glare. Some students who needed more direct illumination brought tiny lights that attached to their desk or book. I asked parents to bring in one or two floor lamps to provide at least one area of indirect light. The students and I

IN THEIR OWN WORDS

I can't concentrate if the light's too bright in class—it gives me a headache.

—Cindy, seventh grade

discussed the alternatives and why lighting is an important factor for some and no big deal for others.

After a recent PTA meeting, a woman came up to me and identified herself as the wife of a highly skilled surgeon. "My husband constantly complains that there's never enough light in the house," she said. "Now I think I understand why. I'm going to go to the medical supply and buy one of those high-powered overhead lights they use in surgery. I'll put it in his home office and maybe at last he'll be happy!"

The solution may not always be that drastic, but you'll be surprised at how much of a difference lighting can make with some children. Even if your kids cannot have any choice at all during the school day, encourage them to experiment with varying degrees of light when they're working at home.

The Homeschool Advantage

If you are teaching your children at home, the chances are good that they are already accustomed to the degree of light you typically utilize. It may not have occurred to you that the issue of light could be affecting anyone's concentration level. Since awareness is at least half the battle, discuss the lighting options with your children and experiment with different kinds and levels of light. If it doesn't make a difference, note that. If it *does* make a difference, challenge your child to design a study space that incorporates the right kind of light along with other important environmental aspects. You may also want to find areas with fluorescent lighting (such as the public library or a cafeteria) where your children can practice dealing with the kind of light that will be illuminating the room where they take standardized tests like the SAT.

STRETCHING THE SHOE

Some Practical and Immediate Adaptations

- Whenever possible, try to get your child to class early enough to choose the seat that offers the best match in lighting needs.
- Design personal lighting for your child's study space at home.
- Add your own ideas:

____

____

____

CHANGING THE SHOE

Some Ideal Solutions

- Provide varied lighting in different areas of the classroom.
- Allow students to bring their own lighting adaptations, within reason, i.e., a visor to diffuse bright lighting, or a personal study lamp to increase the light at their desks.
- Add your own ideas:

____

____

____

TRY IT OUT

Chart your personal preferences for the type of lighting that works best for you while you relax, work, or learn. Then encourage others to chart theirs as well, and compare and discuss.

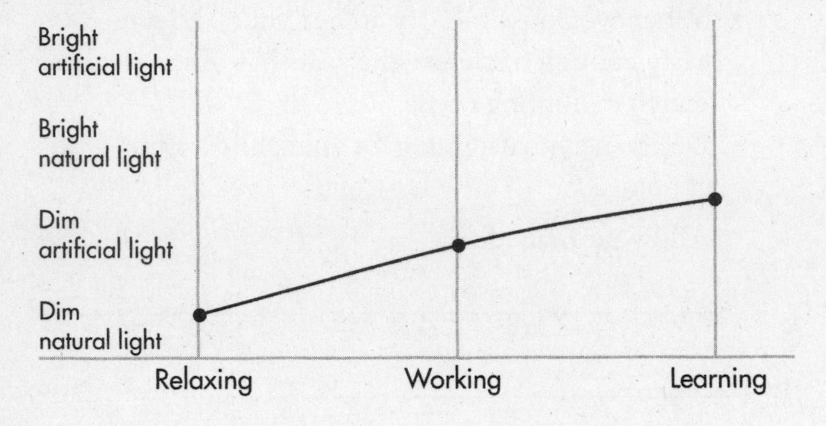

5 Make Yourself Comfortable

Sister Mary believes that students' concentration is triggered when they are permitted to learn in a physical environment conducive to their ability to do their best. Thus, every classroom has both traditional seats and desks and an informal, carpeted area.

—Shirley Griggs and Rita Dunn, *Learning Styles*

Have you sat in a school desk lately? Would you enjoy doing a full day's work there? Let's face it—as adults in the workplace, we make it a point to go out and get the most ergonomically correct and physically comfortable chair available. And yet, year after year in school classrooms across the country, we provide what have to be the most uncomfortable desks available.

Put yourself in that student's place at the standard-issue classroom desk for a moment. If your legs are too short and your feet don't touch the ground, what happens within about five minutes? That's right—your feet start tingling and going to sleep. As you fidget and squirm and try to get the feeling back in them, you get in trouble for not paying attention to the teacher.

Sometimes a solution as simple as putting a cardboard box under a child's feet can relieve the pressure of feet dangling above the floor and do away with a distraction that could have easily led to that student becoming perceived as a behavior problem.

The desks and chairs in a classroom are hard and unforgiving when your back stays pressed against those metal bars for long periods of time. As you twist and stretch and try to get more comfortable, it sure looks to the teacher like you're not paying attention.

Sometimes just putting a small, inflatable travel pillow behind a child's back can make the difference between focusing on what a teacher is saying and becoming preoccupied with how much your back hurts.

Several children have mentioned to me how embarrassing it is to sit in a school desk that is attached to the chair if you're a little bigger than other kids your age. Squeezing into a tight space that doesn't adjust at all is not only physically uncomfortable, but also can be emotionally humiliating. As adults, we simply wouldn't tolerate it.

Many elementary teachers have seen the delight of their students when an old carpeted bathtub became the reading center in the back of the room, but older students are often expected to grow out of such things and learn to sit at a standard desk. There's an unspoken message that if you prefer to sit on the floor or in beanbag chairs or sofas that you're not really taking your class work seriously. The fact is, some of us are just not designed to be comfortable in a rigid desk and chair while we work. If the point of an assignment is to get the work done and I can get it done faster and better if I lie on the floor or sit on a couch, how would it be more productive to force me to sit at a desk?

Many individual teachers have managed to incorporate an informal area in their classrooms despite the lack of official support or budget. There have even been several schools that have encouraged the whole staff to offer some options to students who struggle with formal classroom instruction.

IN THEIR OWN WORDS

Something that would help school make a lot more sense to me would be letting students work in comfortable places.

—Travis, eighth grade

One high school principal in the Dallas, Texas, area made sure his whole staff had the financial support and training to integrate learning styles into their curriculum. Participation was voluntary, but the majority of the teachers elected to spend the time and effort to make it work, even though many had reservations. Both teachers and administrators admitted they were surprised to see how well it worked:

> Initially, many teachers were concerned that they would lose control of their classes if they permitted students to sit informally or work with peers to complete tasks. Others were overwhelmed at the prospect of accommodating a variety of learning styles simultaneously. [Principal] Harp encouraged teachers to experiment with one or two beginning approaches as a means of determining the effectiveness of teaching to student strengths.

> At first teachers thought that basic-skills students would be most amenable to learning styles approaches. However, they found that high achieving students in the extended classes were equally as enthusiastic about the changes initiated as a result of accommodating their individual instructional preferences.
>
> [Teacher Sherrye] Dotson also confided that, prior to the advent of her learning styles program, students would wait in the hall until the last minute before classes began. "Now they come into the room, take their books and materials to wherever they feel most comfortable, and immediately get to work. When I start the lesson, they merely stop what they're doing and begin to interact with me."[5]

One of the most common objections to providing the flexibility of informal classroom design has to do with the potential of so many distractions. Won't kids take advantage of having a couch or beanbag chairs to just kick back and take a nap instead of listening? Not if you hold them accountable. When I first introduced the "cozy corner" in the back of my high school classroom, almost all the students fought over who would get to sit there. I have to admit it was a little chaotic for the first couple of days. But I insisted that everyone who sat on the couch and chairs would have to prove there was an increase in their listening skills and an improvement in the class work they were turning in. It didn't take long for the novelty to wear off for most of them. One by one, I'd hear a student say, "Be quiet—I can't concentrate back here!" or "I'm going to fall asleep if I sit on that couch again."

Within a week, only a few students were consistently sitting in the comfy seats, and those were usually the kids who had really been struggling to pay attention. Now, they were the best listeners in the class.

This doesn't mean that every classroom has to look like an executive airport lounge. It doesn't mean every student has to have plush, comfortable surroundings. Some students actually do concentrate better in a formal, traditional, desk-and-chair environment. For the students who do need some adjustments, the classroom variations don't even have to be that extreme. Most importantly, we need to help the students themselves recognize what kind of physical environment they need in order to concentrate best. Then, even if it's not possible to provide those conditions at school, they will at least know what to look for when they study on their own.

IN THEIR OWN WORDS

I'd like to have desks that have a built-in white board. That way, you can draw and whatnot without wasting paper or destroying the desks.

—Shawn, high school student

Some parents are very uncomfortable letting their children study in nontraditional ways at home. For many, it's hard to believe that a sixteen-year-old girl lying on her stomach on the floor with headphones on, television in the background, drinking a diet cola and munching on a snack mix is actually getting any real work done.

One mother of a fifth-grade girl cornered me after a learning styles seminar. "My daughter says on Thursday nights she can only do her homework between 8 and 8:30 while she watches her favorite television program. I think that's just an excuse."

I replied, "Well, there's one sure way to find out. As long as it's a television show you approve of, go ahead and let her do her homework while she's watching it. But at 8:30, when the program is over, you should collect the homework. If it's done and done well, you can say, 'Wow—I guess you're right. I could never study that way, but it obviously works for you.' If, however, the homework isn't done or isn't done well, you get to say to your daughter, 'Nice try. Obviously it doesn't work, so you'll need to try something else.'"

Accountability should never be sacrificed when you're deciding what students need—the bottom line needs to be *what works.*

IN THEIR OWN WORDS

My idea for school being better would be reclining desks . . . no, I'm serious. If we were comfortable, we could learn better. It works with a comfortable couch. I can always watch TV better and stay focused if I am sitting on a nice couch. A cup holder would be helpful, too, but I won't push it.

—John, twelfth grade

The Homeschool Advantage

Although it should be a lot easier to modify study spaces when your children are learning at home, it's sometimes more stressful for you as the parent. If you're used to an organized, traditional learning environment, it may be very difficult for you to watch your learners lounge on the sofa or lie on the floor while you're teaching them the daily history lesson. But you don't have to do all the compromising. Suggest there be a set amount of time each day when everyone tries working in a more formal setting—a desk, a chair, a table. Even if it's not their favorite place, they'll know it's temporary, and it's good practice for the situations outside home that won't be so accommodating. Remember to hold your children accountable for proving the nonconforming study environment they may prefer actually produces the best results possible.

STRETCHING THE SHOE

Some Practical and Immediate Adaptations

- Provide a small portable fold-up footstool or cardboard box to use as a footstool if you have a child with short legs that don't touch the floor.
- Make small travel-size pillows available for children whose aching backs distract them when sitting in an uncomfortable chair.
- Add your own ideas:

____

____

____

CHANGING THE SHOE

Some Ideal Solutions

- Provide a variety of styles of comfortable and ergonomically correct desks, chairs, and study areas in the classroom.

- Give the students a budget and let them design their own best working space.
- Add your own ideas:

____

____

____

TRY IT OUT

If your student needs a little help in deciding what he or she would need in order to concentrate, here are a few suggested questions:

When passing the test or doing the homework *really* matters:

- Where am I studying?
- When am I studying (time of day)?
- What's in the background (music, room noise, silence)?
- Who's with me (other people, a pet)?
- What, if anything, am I eating or drinking?
- How can I convince my parents to let me try studying this way?

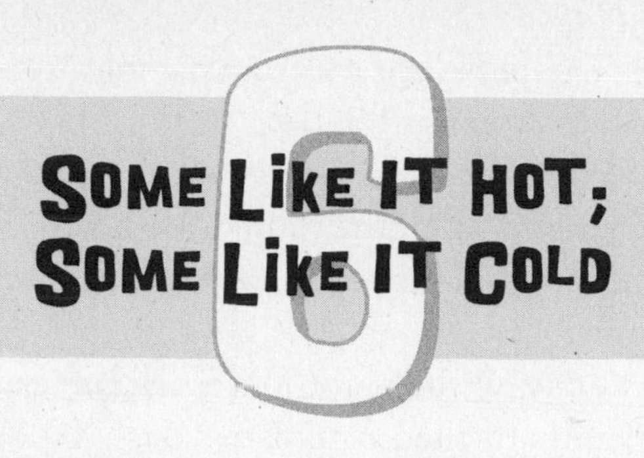

6 Some Like It Hot; Some Like It Cold

Whether . . . personality traits are perceived as problems surely has something to do with the environment in which a person is functioning.

—Dr. Lawrence Diller, *Running on Ritalin*

Sam was probably the most restless student Mrs. M. had in her third grade class. It seemed he was always fidgeting, squirming, daydreaming. Sam had already been held back once in his short educational journey. Despite visits to several different medical and educational professionals, the reasons for his lack of success still remained largely a mystery.

Mrs. M. decided to give her class a quick, informal learning styles profile, so I came in to work with them for a couple of days. I noticed Sam's distraction right away, and we didn't capture his attention until we asked everyone to share what they needed in order to do better in school. His answer to almost every question we asked was somehow related to the temperature of the room.

"I'd concentrate better if the room were cooler."

"Something that keeps me from paying attention to the teacher is . . . the room is too hot."

"Something my teacher needs to know about me is . . . I can't concentrate when the room's too hot."

The teacher and I looked at each other. Could it really be that simple?

The next day, we brought in a small battery-operated clip-on fan and attached it to Sam's desk. As soon as the breeze hit his face, he broke into a wide grin. He took a deep breath, looked expectantly at the teacher—and began to pay attention. While the change in temperature didn't solve all of Sam's attention problems, his teacher noted with surprise that his level of concentration increased dramatically over the next few days.

Fortunately, not every student is as temperature-sensitive as Sam. But for those who are, what if we are overlooking a relatively easy problem to solve? I happen to be a lot like Sam—if I'm too hot, I just can't think about anything else until I get cooler. My physical discomfort clouds everything else, and I lose all ability to concentrate on anything but getting cool. I have a good friend who is just the opposite. She is perpetually cold, and even in the heat of summer, the air conditioning in a building can literally freeze her concentration level. Most people can get over it—they adjust or endure and just keep going. But there are often several students in each

IN THEIR OWN WORDS

I think I'd learn better at school if they would turn the heat down and give us two lunches.

—Carl, sixth grade

classroom who are so sensitive to the room temperature that they can't think of anything else.

There's certainly a geographic element to many temperature preferences, and to a great extent, it can be what you get used to. In the Seattle, Washington, area where we live, we just don't get that many sunny days in the fall and winter. We're used to a cooler climate, so if there's a day with bright sunshine and no clouds, even if it's only 45 degrees, you'll see people putting on their shorts and sandals, sitting outdoors, and dropping the tops of their convertibles.

On the other hand, when I visit southern Florida and the temperatures dip into the mid to high 60s, I'm amazed at the thickness of the sweaters and parkas the native Floridians start wearing.

As minor an issue as it may seem, isn't it conceivable that children who are moved to a climate that's much different than they're used to might have physical discomfort that interferes with their concentration? Isn't it also possible that even children who are comfortable with the outdoor climate could have a built-in thermostat that is at odds with the classroom temperature? If you yourself are a person for whom temperature is not an issue, it may not even occur to you that it could be a significant obstacle for your child.

Most teachers will tell you that they have very little if any control over the temperature of their individual classrooms. Even when a teacher *can* adjust the settings, students are largely at the mercy of the *teacher's* temperature preference. It's usually up to the students themselves to dress comfortably for the environment. Often the students may not even realize how much of an effect the wrong temperature has on their focus and attention span.

Sometimes the best remedy for temperature fluctuation is simply to encourage your children to layer their clothing—a short-sleeve shirt under a sweater under a jacket. If they get too warm, they can gradually take off each layer and stay relatively comfortable. Remember, awareness is usually half the battle, and if children can recognize the obstacles, they're that much closer to figuring out what it will take for them to succeed.

The Homeschool Advantage

The best place to study where you can adjust individual room temperature is almost always at home, so your homeschoolers have a distinct advantage if any of them is particularly temperature sensitive. Remember, it won't be that big a deal to many kids, so it may not even be an issue for you. Discuss the subject with your children, and ask if it's easier for them to study and work in a warm room or a cool room. If they show no preference or they don't know, you can either experiment with different temperatures, or just drop the whole topic and move on to something more important.

> **IN THEIR OWN WORDS**
>
> *One of my top ten complaints about school is that there aren't enough air conditioners.*
>
> *—Luke, fourth grade*

STRETCHING THE SHOE

Some Practical and Immediate Adaptations

- Wear layers of clothing—be sure to have a place to safely store discarded items throughout the day.

- At home, experiment with different temperatures as you work to see if it makes a significant difference.
- Add some of your own ideas:

____

____

____

CHANGING THE SHOE

Some Ideal Solutions

- Provide different areas in the classroom that offer varying degrees of temperature.
- Make safety-certified space heaters or personal fans available for children who really benefit from them.
- Add some of your own ideas:

____

____

____

TRY IT OUT

Try making the classroom setting deliberately warmer or cooler while students are working. Let the students try to figure out what temperature seems to be the best for concentrating and working, keeping in mind that some students really won't have an opinion one way or another.

TIME OUT!

Whether it's public or private schools, we can't really offer a custom-made, private study space for each student according to his or her learning style, right?

We can't totally redesign the schedules of every school so we only require students to take classes during the times that work best for them, can we?

It would take, in some cases, an astronomical amount of money to re-engineer the heating and cooling systems of every school building so that individual classrooms could control their own temperature level, wouldn't it?

Besides, school isn't supposed to be *comfortable,* is it? It's not a place to be pampered and catered to—it's a training ground where you learn discipline and structure, right?

These are certainly very legitimate concerns, and we've heard the same objections for decades. While I don't believe we need to cater to every individual learning style or turn our schools into luxurious "Club Meds," I do think some changes that respect basic human physiology are significantly past due in our current educational institutions. Unless we want our children to suffer simply because we did when *we* were in school, it's time to redesign the classrooms.

PART 2

LEARNING STYLES

7 Look Who's Talking

An auditory child likes to be heard from. If you don't let him talk in the beginning, he is going to interrupt you until he has a chance to talk.

—Walter Barbe, *Growing Up Learning*

In school my least favorite classes were those where the teacher simply lectured and students were required to carefully take notes. When I took education classes as part of my teacher training, it was a commonly accepted idea that *auditory* learners appreciated those lectures most, since they learned best by hearing. It wasn't until I took learning styles classes in graduate school that I discovered the whole truth about students with strong auditory preferences.

Auditory learners *do* learn best by hearing, but *not* by hearing other people talk to them. They learn best by hearing *themselves* talk. Now, that's a whole new ball game—it turns out that the auditory kids are usually the ones who talk too much!

As soon as an auditory learner thinks of something, he tends to start talking about what he's thinking. The teacher has told him a dozen times to raise his hand first—and he means to—but he keeps blurting out the answer. If he can't talk to the teacher, he *has* to talk to *someone*—so he turns and begins whispering to his neighbors, and the whole classroom often starts buzzing.

The teacher begins the lesson by saying, "Today, we're going to talk about animal cruelty—"

"Oh! My aunt—she had this dog—"

"Sarah, we don't have time for everyone to share a personal story. Let's just go ahead and listen and maybe we'll have time to hear your example at the end of the lesson."

IN THEIR OWN WORDS

I need to discuss things—I like a comfortable place where I can express my ideas verbally. I can also move around and make noise if I need to.

—Megan, high school student

One problem: Sarah now has her aunt's dog story right on the tip of her tongue. All the words have crowded their way up her throat and there's no room for any new words to go the other direction. As the teacher keeps talking, Sarah can't even focus on what she's saying until she can tell someone her story.

As parents and teachers, it seems like we spend a lot of time trying to keep kids quiet. But the fact is, highly auditory learners don't learn much unless they can *talk*. As soon as they hear themselves say the words, the concepts or facts begin to make sense and can be remembered. One very valuable strategy I discovered when teaching adults *or* children is to take periodic breaks of a minute or so as I'm teaching and have the students compare the notes they've taken, discuss what might have occurred to them, or ask someone around them a clarification question. The interruption is very brief—some teachers even turn over an egg timer so the class has a visual reminder—and the group almost instantly gives me their attention again as soon as I ask for it. They don't need a lot of time—just a few moments to talk about what they're thinking or learning.

Over the years, I've found that if *I* am the one who provides several opportunities where students are actually encouraged to talk, they almost always talk about what I'm teaching them. Not only that, but they're remembering more information when the session is over, because—for the auditory learners especially—they didn't have to hold on to their own thoughts while trying to make room for new ones. When the conversation level becomes enthusiastic and animated, I usually take it as a great compliment, not as a sign I'm losing control.

IN THEIR OWN WORDS

Something that would help school make a lot more sense to me would be to have more class discussions rather than just getting an assignment and doing it.

—Francis, eighth grade

Many auditory learners don't even realize they are talking out loud. As researcher Walter Barbe points out in his book *Growing Up Learning,* "Your auditory child is a talker. He is the one who might disturb other students in his class by reading his lesson out loud when he thinks he is reading to himself. He needs to hear what he is reading in order to learn it."[6] We've discovered that many auditory students tend to be slower readers—not slow because they can't read well, but slow because they have to hear the *sound* of every word they read. If they can't read aloud, they still read aloud to themselves in their own heads, and when they come across a word they don't know how to pronounce, they may just stop. If there are lots of technical words, or even nonsensical, made-up words, the auditory reader may become too frustrated to continue. For a long time, many have believed that auditory learners like the book-on-tape option because they can listen to someone read to them. Although for most that's still true, it's even more beneficial because the auditory listener can hear the rhythm and flow and sound of the written words.

When you give directions or instructions to an auditory learner, you will often hear your words repeated back to you like an echo. Until the listener hears herself say the words, she often can't remember what was said. An auditory kid may get labeled as a "chatterbox," because from the moment she walks in the door after school, she begins to recount every detail of her day, share every thought she's currently having, and talk about her plans for the rest of the evening. If you happen to be a parent who doesn't share such a high auditory preference, it can be exhausting to listen to an almost nonstop flow of words that may or may not fit together in any reasonable sequence. Your auditory child may be disappointed in your response because you don't talk nearly as much as she does. Walter Barbe has a good observation and suggestion for parents of an auditory child.

> If she cannot talk and listen to others talking, she may not learn as much as she is able. At home, nonauditory

> parents may want a period of "peace and quiet" only to find themselves repeatedly harassed by questions, requests, stories, and announcements. Try giving your child your undivided listening attention for a set period of time. When you need your time for quiet, channel her audition by suggesting she make up stories with her animals and dolls. Or put on a record or tape for her to listen to.[7]

Sometimes an auditory learner doesn't actually talk that much. Instead, he may almost constantly be making some sort of "thinking noise." He's tapping his pencil, humming, or making another noise that may be driving his parents or teachers crazy. "Can't you for five minutes *stop making that noise?*" What noise? Usually he doesn't even realize he's making a noise—he's thinking, and in order to think he makes his noise. Mind you, he can't think with anybody *else's* noise—everyone else has to stop making noise!

IN THEIR OWN WORDS

If I don't understand something after hearing it the first time, I really need to ask questions until I do.

—Taylor, sixth grade

Teachers worry about keeping control in a classroom if too many students are talking too often. There's no doubt that in some cases, students are not paying attention because they are too busy talking. But we may be overlooking the fact that many of those auditory students are talking because they *were* paying attention. We cannot assume that all talking and interaction among the students in a classroom is automatically a negative thing. As a teacher, I believe I should be less focused on keeping all my students from talking and much more focused on giving them important facts and concepts to talk *about*. This doesn't mean we should just let students talk anytime they feel like it—there should definitely still be accountability. But we also shouldn't believe that just because all the children in a classroom are quiet they're actually learning anything.

The Homeschool Advantage

If you are a homeschool parent with a low tolerance for noise and disruption, you may become very frustrated with your auditory child. You may not welcome a constant stream of conversation, questions, and interruptions. If, on the other hand, you as a *parent* are a very auditory learner, you may actually be more frustrated with your children who are *not* as auditory. When you ask for input or want to discuss a concept or idea, you may find your nonauditory child is frustratingly quiet and seemingly unresponsive. Either way, the chances are good there will be some misunderstandings. If your auditory child needs more opportunities to talk and you don't feel comfortable with the interaction, look for ways you can help your child talk without you—study buddies, tape recorders, and so on. Ask questions more often, and let your auditory student tell you about what he or she is reading or studying. When you hand your child a sheet with instructions or directions on it, read through it aloud together. When you give praise or correction, say it out loud so your auditory child can process it more quickly. For spelling, try having your auditory learner dictate the spelling words, letter by letter, as you write them on a piece of paper or on a white board. Most importantly, talk to all your children about learning style differences, and look for ways to bring out the strengths in each other without sacrificing any bottom-line outcomes.

STRETCHING THE SHOE

Some Practical and Immediate Adaptations

- Help your auditory child cope by thinking of ways to keep from talking out of turn in class. For example, when something occurs to him while the teacher is talking, suggest he jot down a quick note to himself to ask about or discuss later.
- Find someone at home who will help your auditory child get started working by letting her talk through what she needs to do.
- Add your own ideas:

___

___

___

CHANGING THE SHOE

Some Ideal Solutions

- Provide frequent opportunities for students to briefly share and discuss with each other what they just learned.
- Have a "study buddy" for each student who wants one; encourage students to use each other as sounding boards to help figure out how to do assignments.

- Add your own ideas:

____

____

____

TRY IT OUT

If you've been frustrated with a child who seems to talk too much, try finding as many opportunities as possible to let that child verbalize his or her thoughts and questions. In the classroom, it actually works pretty well to simply turn over a one-minute egg timer and let the students interact with each other after each important concept is taught. When they know they won't have to wait very long before they can share what they're thinking, it's surprising how quietly they can listen. At home, instead of simply tuning them out, let your auditory children talk about their day right away, and talk through what they need to do in the way of homework assignments. Use phrases like "Let's talk about it," "Repeat after me," and "Tell me what you think it says."

If you get tired of hearing your auditory child talk, try asking for the short version of the story, or perhaps adopt the use of a code word that can signal when it's really important to listen. Most importantly, instead of constantly insisting your auditory child be quiet, look for ways to verbalize learning, and talk through problems or important issues.

8 I See What You Mean

If you are visual, you probably do not talk at length, nor do you listen for extended periods of time without looking off, staring into space, or finding some focus for your attention. . . . The most effective means for your spouse or child to remind you about something is to write notes and leave them in a spot you will be sure to notice.

—Walter Barbe, *Growing Up Learning*

If you've ever gotten in trouble in school for daydreaming, you were probably using your visual learning strengths without even realizing it. When we think of visual learners, most of us think of those who need visual aids, such as pictures, overheads, flannelgraph stories, and Power Point presentations. Although that's true, there's much more to being a visual learner than even the teacher education classes taught us.

When you're a highly visual learner, like I am, you also have an active—and sometimes overactive—visual imagination. As soon as someone starts talking to you, you get a picture. Okay, it might not be the *right* picture, but you definitely have a picture. And as you sit there in class, thinking about the visual image in your head, you often get further and further away from what the teacher is actually saying. In fact, many parents and teachers might be horrified if they could peer into little heads and see the pictures that visual children have to go with what the adults *thought* was so clearly communicated.

I do a lot of flying, and on one particular airline on one specific type of aircraft, there's a sign on the outside of the tiny, pillbox airplane bathroom. The sign says, *No Smoking in Toilet*. I asked a flight attendant, "How could that even be possible?" He didn't get it. "Well," he began, "we have smoke alarms—" "No, no," I interrupted. "I mean, I'm a tall person. I couldn't even *fit* in the toilet." He still didn't get it. I tried again. "And what about those signs on the back of every seat that say *Fasten Seat Belt While Seated*—how could you do it any other way?" He just shook his head and looked at me like I was crazy. But my visual mind quickly attaches a mental image to the written words on signs—and the result is probably rarely what the sign maker had in mind.

When I see a sign that says, *Bowling Animal Clinic,* even though Dr. Bowling is probably a fine veterinarian, I can't help but wonder whether the animals are bowling, or being bowled *with*. When the sign on the back of the door in the doctor's exam room says, *Please leave door open when exiting,* I'm trying to figure out how anyone but Casper the Friendly Ghost could get out *without* leaving it open. Not long ago, I was at the checkout counter at a Christian bookstore when I saw a display box of Shalom, a small, travel-size bottle of hand lotion. On the side of the box, it proclaimed: *The fine fragrance of ancient Israel*. I had to ask the clerk. "Does that mean it smells like the camel dung and unwashed *bodies* in ancient Israel?" She gave me an exasperated look. "No," she said impatiently. "It means frankincense and myrrh." I nodded, but persisted. "I surely can't be the only person who thinks the fragrance of *ancient* Israel is not particularly appealing." She put her hands on her hips and replied, "Nobody thinks like you."

Yes, they do! Many of you reading this right now understand how my visual mind works—and you could add dozens of examples to the ones above. The offbeat images often find their way into my visual mind unbidden, but once I have a picture, it's almost impossible to erase it. There are many kids like me sitting in a classroom, listening and trying to picture what's really being taught. If you don't check in with us periodically, if you don't ask us, "What do you picture when I say that?" or "Do you see what I mean?" you may not even realize it when we drift off into our visual "daydream world" and stop trying to grasp what you're teaching.

IN THEIR OWN WORDS

I think I'd study better if the homework sheets had more pictures to help me understand what they mean.

—Adam, seventh grade

No one is exclusively a visual learner—but many of us have a rather large piece of that puzzle. Visual learners often have, in many ways, an easier time in school just from the standpoint of how many visual demands the classroom and homework make. Reading is primarily visual; worksheets, handouts, and lessons on the blackboard or overhead rely on visual memory. There are some areas, however, that are almost biased *against* visual learners. The classic example is the traditional spelling bee. Even though I'm an excellent speller, I cannot usually spell a word by simply saying it. If I can write it down and look at it, I can almost always spell it correctly. If the teacher gives me directions verbally and doesn't have them in writing, the chances are good the information will go in one ear, gain speed, and go out the other. It isn't that I'm not paying attention; I just don't have anything to focus on visually, and that puts me at a distinct disadvantage.

When it comes to reading, often the more visual learners can really struggle with phonics. Walter Barbe's research demonstrates there may be a very good reason.

> If the teaching strategy concentrates on phonics—either in the book, with the teacher or both—your visual child may run into trouble, for he cannot relate purely auditory material to the words without a strong visual model. He may read perfectly well but not do well in phonics exercises. He should not be forced to learn reading through phonics, but rather be allowed to use visual imagery and a sight approach.[8]

Sometimes, when students fall behind in their phonics lessons, we place them in "remedial" reading groups where we are guilty of simply teaching phonics slower and louder. Phonics seems to work very well for children who are more auditory, but we know there are many children who are much more visual. Rather than insist that phonics be the *only* method of teaching reading, we should offer a sight word approach as well—remembering that the whole point is that *the child learns to read*. I'm not talking about lowering any standards or letting kids get by without learning to read—I'm talking about defining the goal and finding the best way we can to help every child succeed in reaching it.

Unless they are also highly auditory, visual learners probably won't be a problem when it comes to talking out of turn. They usually prefer to watch and observe more than comment and discuss. Teachers and parents alike may sometimes find it difficult to engage the visual learner in conversation, since it makes more sense to see something before you talk about it. When I was a classroom teacher, I found it effective to occasionally do a "ticket out the door" exercise. Each student wrote a response to a question on a piece of paper that they then handed to me as they walked out the door. The questions were short and simple: "What was the most frustrating part of your assignment today?" or "What part of school do you look forward to the most?" or "Why do you think some students consider poetry to be boring?" Students who would normally not have said anything to me in front of the class often felt much freer to express themselves in writing.

IN THEIR OWN WORDS

School should be drastically shortened. I spend 90 percent of the time staring out the window.

—Joel, twelfth grade

Many parents want to get more information from their kids about how school went than the traditional response "fine." You might try putting a small white board on the front of the refrigerator or somewhere else in the kitchen with two columns on it: "The best thing about my day was . . ." and "The worst thing about my day was . . ." Often the more visual child will write notes or draw pictures to communicate what she is thinking or feeling. Don't push for daily or detailed responses—in the beginning, at least, be happy with a sentence or two and watch for more as time goes by.

Often visual learners may appear distracted in class. Before we automatically assume they just aren't listening, we need to understand that they need to see things in their own mind's eye. Sometimes they draw or doodle while they listen; sometimes they avoid looking at the speaker because they need to focus on the image they have of what's being taught. After delivering a forty-five-minute keynote at a high school student leaders' conference in Ohio, I was approached by the student body president from one of the larger high schools. He was holding his handout packet, but had turned it over to the blank page on the back. There he had drawn an incredibly detailed picture. "Mrs. Tobias," he said, "I wanted to show you the picture that I drew while you were talking." He proudly showed me the picture, and I hesitantly took it in my hand for a closer look. I tried to sound enthusiastic as I complimented him. "That's a great picture—very nice." He looked closer at me. "You're thinking I wasn't listening, aren't you?" he asked. Before I could reply, he continued. "If you asked me any question about anything you talked about in the last forty-five minutes, I would look at this picture and be able to answer it. It's all in here." I must have looked a little surprised, but he then made his point. "The trouble is, my whole life teachers have said, 'I want all eyes up here—put your pens and pencils down and look at me.'" He shrugged. "If I can't draw or doodle while I listen, I can't remember very well."

Interesting, isn't it? Here we've been thinking that if students doodle in the margins or draw on their papers and don't look at the teacher, they're not paying attention. Sometimes they're not. But sometimes they're drawing in *order* to pay attention. For a lot of highly visual learners, they are actually better off if they *don't* look at the teacher the whole time.

> **IN THEIR OWN WORDS**
>
> *If I don't understand something after hearing it the first time, I really need to have someone do it while I watch.*
>
> *—Kathy, sixth grade*

Visual learners like to use bright, colorful items to organize and store just about anything. Within reason, provide the visual learner with the most up-to-date and pleasing-to-the-eye binders, folders, pencil boxes, and so on. The danger is, of course, that the visual learner can count on the system to organize itself and not realize it is only as effective as the person who is using it.

The Homeschool Advantage

Your visual homeschooler is often the perfect person to help you design charts, graphs, and illustrations for lessons, chores, and schedules. Take advantage of the drawing, doodling, and daydreaming to find ways your child can get credit for doing assignments and projects. Instead of insisting that everything be written out, look for opportunities for your child to use pictures or designs to supplement the worksheets or even tests. Don't be afraid to try alternate methods of teaching reading or spelling or math using more visual strategies. Remember, the most important question to ask is, What's the point? If you know what your child needs in the way of knowledge or skills, you can find many visual ways for him to demonstrate he has learned it.

STRETCHING THE SHOE

Some Practical and Immediate Adaptations

- Suggest your child try putting sticky notes on the pages of books or worksheets and use them for drawing or doodling pictures or notes to help him remember.
- Just for fun, help your visual child keep a list of favorite images or mental pictures of words, phrases, signs, and so on.
- Add your own ideas:

____

____

____

CHANGING THE SHOE

Some Ideal Solutions

- Provide opportunities for students to draw and/or describe visual pictures of the concepts they are taught.
- Encourage creative and imaginative applications of basic principles and seemingly "boring" tasks and concepts.
- Add your own ideas:

____

____

____

TRY IT OUT

If you have a child who seems to be a daydreamer, try experimenting with more visual methods of studying and remembering. Ask your child questions like "What do you picture when you hear that?" or "What do you think the assignment should look like?" You might want to try flash cards for remembering facts, vocabulary, or spelling words, but encourage your visual child to design his *own* flash cards. After all, the picture he has in his mind may be very different from the one on standard-issue visual aids. Instead of fighting your child's urge to doodle and draw, allow her to use a pen or pencil while you talk as long as she can prove she was actually listening.

On The Move

Teachers will recognize kinesthetic learners as the ones who are always asking to go to the bathroom and to sharpen their pencils, two of the only acceptable reasons for moving around during class time.

—Walter Barbe, *Growing Up Learning*

What are you doing right now while you're reading this book? Are you sitting still? Are you really? The chances are good that you *are* moving in some way—no matter how subtle. Almost everyone finds themselves moving when they think and learn; it's just that some people have an extra dose of that restless energy that especially gets you in trouble when you are younger. These kids hear the same things over and over as they're growing up: "Put your feet on the floor!" "Sit still!" "No—you're not going to the bathroom again; you've been there three times already!" "No—no more drinks—sit down!" It's not unusual to see several parents actually sitting on various parts of their child's body to keep him from moving in church or other public places.

The fact is, some children are just more kinesthetic—that is, *born* to move. If you take an active, born-to-move child and make her sit still while you teach her, what will she be thinking about while you're talking? That's right—moving, and the fact that she can't. So what's the point? The school classroom is one of the only places in your life you will be where you will be told you can't move. Sure, you have to be motionless when your blood pressure is taken or during certain medical procedures—but other than that, you're free to at least scratch your nose, twitch your feet, stretch your arms, and so on. Why is it so important that children sit perfectly still in their seats while they are taught by the teacher? As a former classroom teacher, I believe that wanting students to sit still is mostly for *our* convenience. It's easier to stand up in front of a group of students and speak to them if they're quiet and still. I like it when they sit in rapt attention, looking directly at me, drinking in my every word. But I learned early in my teaching career that that type of listening doesn't happen very often. It also makes a better impression if your principal drops in or a parent stops by for a visit. It somehow appears you have more control over your class when they sit still and look at you.

IN THEIR OWN WORDS

Something that would help school make a lot more sense to me would be not to have to sit and listen to the teacher. Why not stand up?

—Jennifer, sixth grade

Highly kinesthetic students are often the first to be labeled "hyperactive." They draw attention to themselves because of their energy, their movement, and their restless spirit. It's difficult for such active students to sit in small desks and write in small spaces and listen for long periods of time. For an overwhelming number of kids (and adults, for that matter), being able to move when they learn will determine how much they remember. They need to get their hands on stuff, convert concepts into action, experiment with ideas, and *do* something with the facts they're given. If this sounds like dealing with these kids might be inconvenient for the busy adults in their lives, you're right. Fortunately, many adults share this strong kinesthetic preference and can offer more opportunities for alternatives to the motionless, sterile classroom. But these educators are still in the minority, and school continues to be a confining and sometimes physically painful place to be for highly active students. Dr. Peter Breggin states that "the acceptable norm may be at fault in expecting energetic, curious children to sit still and shut up for hours at a time in group classrooms."[9] He quotes John Holt, an author and educator who went before a committee investigating the process of labeling children with ADHD (Attention Deficit Hyperactivity Disorder). Holt asked how we can determine when a child's energy level should be considered a "disease":

> The answer is simple. We consider it a disease because it makes it difficult to run our schools as we do, like maximum security prisons, for the comfort and convenience of the teachers and administrators who work in them. The energy of children is "bad" because it is a nuisance to the exhausted and overburdened adults who do not want to or know how to and are not able to keep up with it.[10]

Fortunately, many teachers are finding effective ways to use their kinesthetic children's strengths in ways that actually help them pay attention. Some teachers have given highly active students *two* assigned seats—one in the front of the class and one in the back. As long as they are sitting in one or the other and are not distracting the rest of the kids when they move, they can switch seats as often as they need to. Other teachers have gotten permission to put two or three rocking chairs in the back of the classroom. The most restless students can elect to sit in the rocking chairs as long as they can prove that sitting in them helps them listen better and learn more. Several teachers have adopted more subtle methods of accommodating their kinesthetic learners by providing a soft, cushiony ball for the child to squeeze while listening, or letting them hold on to something like a "worry stone" or a small amount of clay while listening. The point of paying attention in class isn't whether or not students move too much—the point is whether moving can actually help some of them listen better.

IN THEIR OWN WORDS

If I don't understand something after hearing it the first time, I really need to make a dance or song out of it or talk about it with my friends.

—Sally, fourth grade

Reading can pose some difficult challenges for the kinesthetic child. Reading itself is a very visual task, and although a more auditory learner can benefit by reading aloud or being read to, the kinesthetic child is being asked not only to sit still, but to quietly look at words without doing anything else. It's no wonder these children seem to so quickly grow bored. Researcher Walter Barbe suggests actually encouraging those students to use their fingers when they read:

> Finger pointing is a strategy which helps the kinesthetic child focus on the appropriate word. This has often been discouraged but our research shows that pointing, preferably with the index and middle finger, really helps. The width of two fingers "underlines" whole words, rather than single letters, and involves the child physically in the act of reading. Writing letters on her big blackboard and drawing imaginary letters in the air will also help.[11]

Barbe also points out that sometimes the kinesthetic child picks up a book just to turn the pages, which is just fine. Then when your child *does* sit still long enough to read a story, be sure you've chosen books with lots of action right from the beginning. Provide lots of space for sitting and reading, with room to move around. By making a few relatively minor adjustments, you can make sure that your child doesn't view reading as a punishment.

More often than not, some of the most kinesthetic kids in school are student athletes. They can learn to use their bodies with skill and ease on the soccer field or basketball court, but when they come back into the math classroom everything changes. The strengths that helped them succeed as athletes are now seen only as distractions from learning. They must fold themselves into a small desk in a confined space and set aside what often makes them most successful. It's no wonder that their frustration level makes it so hard to concentrate on many academic subjects.

The Homeschool Advantage

One of the best aspects of teaching kinesthetic students at home is the ever-present possibility of field trips. Without a strict time schedule to meet, you have some wonderful opportunities to let your children put action with the words they learn. Challenge the students themselves to find appropriate field trips associated with what they are learning. Teach them how to locate museums, businesses, and other community resources that offer tours or exhibits that can help make the concepts they read in their textbooks more real.

When it comes to designing their space for studying and learning at home, give them free rein in at least one room where they can spread out and work with plenty of space. Remember, the point of the space is to facilitate learning, so if it's just messy and scattered without resulting in the child doing better work, you need to challenge your learner to keep trying out different areas until he finds one that really works.

IN THEIR OWN WORDS

Something that would help school make a lot more sense to me would be four days a week of school then one sports day with sports and recess all day.

—Chase, third grade

STRETCHING THE SHOE

Some Practical and Immediate Adaptations

- Help your active child challenge himself to find ways to move in class that don't get him in trouble, i.e., highlighting notes, holding on to an eraser, or squeezing a "kush ball."

- Encourage your child to find ways of incorporating movement while doing homework or reviewing for a test—i.e., shooting hoops, climbing stairs, and so on—while memorizing spelling words, vocabulary, and other assignments.

- Add your own ideas:

____

____

____

CHANGING THE SHOE

Some Ideal Solutions

- Provide a variety of ways students can move while they are listening, including rocking chairs for some of the most restless ones.
- Redesign school desks with expandable "wings" for more writing space. Let those students who benefit by it work with clipboards and stand or walk around instead of sitting at a desk.

- Add your own ideas:

____

____

____

TRY IT OUT

Try to remember how impractical it is to expect any child to sit perfectly still. Look for even the most subtle ways you can help your child move—in *and* out of school—without getting in trouble for distracting others. Encourage your highly active child to keep finding new outlets for his energy—running errands, taking the stairs, working on the run. There's nothing magic about sitting at a desk to get your work done. Help your child find what works best when it comes to accomplishing a task, even if it's not done in the traditional way. Try practicing sitting still with your child for short periods of time so that when it's really important, she'll be able to do it, at least for a while.

TIME OUT!

So students remember in different ways—what happens to structure, discipline, and accountability?

I'm not a mind reader, but I can't help thinking that some of you reading this book are saying, "Okay, this all makes sense—but you can't just let students talk whenever they feel like it. You can't let them daydream and doodle and not look at you when you're teaching. You can't just let kids get up and walk around when they want to. You have to have discipline and structure in a classroom."

That's right—I absolutely agree. But here's what several teachers and homeschool parents have tried with great success—it's called "The Ten Minute Trial":

You set up several different opposite-case scenarios. For example, "Okay, for the next ten minutes, we're going to work in total silence. But the ten minutes after that, you can talk or have music in the background. Then you need to figure out which way worked best."

Or, "For the next ten minutes, we're going to sit at the desk and work. But the ten minutes after that, you can lie on the floor, sit on the couch, or whatever. Then decide which way made it easier for you to concentrate."

Or, "During the next ten minutes, we're not going to move around at all while we work. But the ten minutes after that, you can move around, sit in a rocking chair, or work with a clipboard. Then figure out which way was more productive for you."

This "Ten-Minute Trial" does two major things. (Bear in mind "ten minutes" can be literal or figurative.) First of all, it lets kids know: "This is not your ten minutes. This ten minutes belongs to someone else, and it's important that we value and respect other people's ten minutes. You might have to wait for one or two or more 'other people's ten minutes' before it gets to be yours." Secondly, and I believe most importantly, it lets kids know that it's important to identify and recognize what *your* "ten minutes" looks like. At some point, you'll have the freedom to study and learn and work independently. If you don't know what your "ten minutes" looks like, if you don't know what it takes to help yourself concentrate and remember, you won't really be an effective lifelong learner.

One of the unexpected benefits I found from using this approach with my students was that it really depersonalized a lot of conflict between us. In the middle of a lesson, a student might raise his hand and say, "This is definitely not my ten minutes. In fact, this whole last *hour* hasn't been my ten minutes. I'm beginning to wonder if it will *ever* be my ten minutes!" And we were both smiling. I wasn't assuming he was criticizing my teaching, and he wasn't assuming he was too dumb to keep up with my instruction. I freely admitted to the students that when I was in school I struggled with chemistry class. "That whole *semester* was *so* not my ten minutes!" But there's something about being aware of *why* we're frustrated that lets us handle the whole situation better.

I know the world will not be giving any of us our own sixty minutes out of every hour. There are many situations where we simply have to learn to deal with uncomfortable and frustrating circumstances that are not bringing out the best in us. But somehow just knowing what we need when we get the chance makes the discipline of not always doing things our way more bearable. The amazing thing is, most of my students who had to operate outside of their most comfortable ten minutes actually seemed to learn more and be more cooperative instead of resenting the idea of being challenged.

In the end, if we can teach our students how to *learn* what we're teaching them, we are sending them out into the world as lifelong learners, not just students who figured out how to survive until they could escape.

10 What's Your Focus?

It's easiest to concentrate on and store things you find exciting, but it is also the case that someone gets interested in things that come together in his brain most readily, making the most sense in his kind of mind.

—Mel Levine, M.D., *A Mind at a Time*

I can walk out of church after an inspiring sermon and say to my friend, "It was wonderful—just what I needed to hear!" She asks, "What was it about?" That stops me in my tracks. "I already told you—it was just what I needed to hear." I didn't know I was going to have to tell anyone what it was *about*. If I had known that before I went into church, I would have listened in a whole different way. I can pay attention to details—if I know which details I'm supposed to pay attention *to*. My natural bent when I listen to a speaker is to absorb in general what's being said, not to focus in on specific points. If I don't know what I'll be asked when it's over, I can appear to be distracted at best and, at worst, to have some sort of attention problem. But it's really more a matter of my learning style than my intelligence.

Dr. Herman Witkin was a psychologist during World War II when he was first hired by the United States Navy. In the course of doing experiments with fighter pilots, Witkin stumbled upon some unexpected findings about how our individual minds are wired. In a nutshell, he found that not everyone was born to be an inherently independent, logical, analytical thinker. There are at least as many of us who are actually born on the other end of the continuum—whose minds are designed with a natural tendency to look for the big picture, to see things in context, to recognize relationships. Over the course of several decades, Witkin and other researchers have also documented the fact that intelligence comes in both extremes—and everything in between. Although our society, and certainly our formal education system, seems to value a predominantly analytical mind-set, those who possess more global traits are also very bright and capable—but they use their intelligence much more intuitively.

In this chapter when I talk about "analytics" and "globals" I am deliberately illustrating the extremes. Of course, no one is *only* global or purely analytic—we all have both pieces of the puzzle. Most students will have one piece that is bigger than the other, but some will be almost even. It's not important that you accurately identify a particular child's style—it's more important that you notice how they are communicating with you and what they seem to value most in any given situation. Most students will display a pattern of learning style behaviors that will be relatively easy to identify. When it comes to school, there are several areas where you can recognize distinct differences between the more analytic and more global learners: in class, in following directions, and in organization.

In Class

Globals listen in different ways than their analytic counterparts do. Analytics seem to automatically tune in on details, listening for the logical sequence of points and events. They are always aware there will be a test later, and they do their best not to miss any important detail. Globals, on the other hand, often listen for things that weren't even said. I can still remember in my high school science class when my teacher told us, "Today we're going to talk about Einstein's Special Theory of Relativity." I remember thinking: *Wow—how did he think of something like that? Where was his laboratory—did he lease office space or have it in his garage? Did Einstein ever marry or have children? What did they think of his theories?* By the time my mind had asked several of these kinds of questions and I finally tuned back in to the lecture, I was startled to realize it had wandered. *Uh-oh—I think I've missed some really important stuff*. I turned to the student next to me and before I could even ask, he said, "Why don't you just *listen?* What's the *matter* with you?" You see, I thought I *was* listening. It's not like I was talking or anything—I just didn't realize my global, big-picture mind had distracted me, made me think about the context and background of the subject, and made me look stupid—again.

IN THEIR OWN WORDS

Something that would help school make a lot more sense to me would be to work every detail out bit by bit.

—Mike, fourth grade

The analytic listens for details right away, and is often frustrated if a teacher seems to be telling too many stories or giving too many examples. Analytic students are frequently raising their hands asking: "Is this going to be on the test?" "Should I write this down?" "Will we need to know this?" They want to make sure they don't miss anything important. When the teacher is lecturing, analytics are happiest when facts and concepts can be broken down from the whole picture into smaller parts that will make sense on their own.

When I was teaching, I loved spelling. I usually managed to think of a clever way to remember how to spell tricky words, and before I knew much about learning styles, I just figured all my students would benefit from my methods. One of the words people often misspell is *cemetery,* commonly putting *ary* at the end instead of *ery*. I had a great idea: Remember when you were little and your mom played with your toes? "This little piggy went to market, this little piggy stayed home." What did the littlest piggy do? That's right, went "wee wee wee" all the way home. Well, this little piggy cried "'E! E! E!' all the way through the cemetery."

Immediately an analytic student's hand went up. "I don't understand what a pig would be *doing* in the cemetery," he said, with a puzzled expression on his face. Exasperated, I replied, "Well, why don't you just *forget* it, then!" He shrugged. "No offense—I just have a harder time remembering your stories than I do memorizing the words. Could I just have a list of words with no tricks?" You see, as a global, I thought that would be so boring! Surely no one would just want a simple, sterile list with no colorful hints!

But one man's boredom is often another man's security, and I learned an important lesson that day. My analytic students had a hard time tuning in to what I was saying when I embellished it with too many stories or took too many "bird walks" by following the inspiration of the moment.

Following Directions

For an analytic learner, following directions—whether it's how to get to the grocery store or how to do a classroom assignment—is easy as long as the directions are given in an analytic manner, step by step, clearly and concisely. If analytics aren't sure what to do, they need to know where to look for more information. For globals, it's just the opposite. Following directions is only easy if they are given with recognizable landmarks or put in context with something the globals already know. Analytic learners can usually understand instructions the first time. After all, their minds are already keyed into details and steps. It's frustrating for them to have to hear the instructions repeated, and yet globals almost always need to hear them twice. For the globals, listening to directions the first time lets them have the big picture; they know what it is they are supposed to do. They need to hear them a second time in order to remember how to do it—the details don't make sense until the big picture is in place.

If globals aren't sure what to do, they don't want to know where to look—they want to know who to ask! The written word doesn't mean much without the personal touch of someone who already knows what they're doing. I freely admit I'm pretty global. Even now, I often pull out a memo from my mailbox and ask, "What does this say?" My analytic husband may ask me, "Why don't you just *read* it?" I *can* read it, of course, but it doesn't mean much to me without hearing another person's interpretation of it. I wasn't the kid who bought a new game and read the inside of the box lid for the rules. I just went over to another kid's house who already knew how to play the game. We'd sit at the table, walk through it a few times, and if we ran into a problem, some analytic would look it up on the box lid! I've never once read a software manual. I stick the disc in, mess with it awhile, and if I can't understand it, I call the toll-free number. A friendly technician on the other end sometimes asks me an obvious question: "Have you read chapter 5?" I reply, "No—I don't really *need* all of chapter 5. If you could just answer this one question for me, I'd be really grateful." I'm not dumb—but I'm also not nearly analytic enough to want to read that manual.

IN THEIR OWN WORDS

If I don't understand something after hearing it the first time, I really need to ask a friend to put it in kid words.

—Victoria, fourth grade

Organization

"Robert, this progress report says you are getting a D in your favorite subject because you have *five* missing assignments!"

"But, Mom, they're right here in my backpack!"

"Your backpack? Why haven't you turned them in?"

"Uh—I thought I did."

This is probably a familiar conversation if you have a highly global child. Remember, a global learner works in big pictures, overall ideas, and spontaneous inspiration. Out of sight, out of mind—and even though we really mean to get better at remembering what our parents and teachers consider the important stuff, it somehow keeps escaping us. Contrary to popular belief, it's not usually because of some neurological disorder—we just have lots of things going on in our brains at the same time.

Most analytic kids prefer to keep their belongings, especially schoolwork, in a neat and orderly manner. They like organization and seem to be able to sort and categorize without much effort. There is a place for everything, and even when some things are out of place, the analytic knows where they need to be. Interestingly enough, if something is missing, it is often the global who can find it. After all, for the analytics, if it's not where it belongs, it is lost. The globals can remember where they last saw it, or think about where they'd be if they *were* it.

If your analytic student is struggling with organization, it's likely she is frustrated with having to do too many things at once. She has a need for structure and order, and if too many tasks must be completed at once, or if there is a lot of chaos in her environment, she cannot function effectively. She needs to at least have input into how her belongings will be organized, and where she will keep what is most important to retrieve. If you want to help her, try giving her more time and space to organize in a way that makes sense to her. Encourage her to find a system that works, and then try to provide her with whatever she needs to maintain it.

If your global student is struggling to be organized, the chances are great that he is more concerned with people than things. He may feel guilty for what his backpack or room look like, but if it comes to making a choice between cleaning and sorting or spending time with a friend, there's no contest. He can be easily distracted from tasks by anyone who asks for his attention, since he'd rather do just about anything than work by himself. If you want to help him, try working with him when he has to clean his room or sort through his backpack. It's not that you have to do much of the work—you just need to be there to help him stay focused on the task at hand.

What's Easiest and Most Difficult about School?

I've talked to hundreds of students from first grade through college age, and they've had very consistent answers when it came to what was easy at school and what took more effort. The analytics agreed that anything easy in school involved structure, organization, and detail. They liked a class syllabus, an outline, detailed notes, clear grading guidelines, independent assignments, and objective tests. They cringed at the thought of group projects, role play, and impromptu changes in plans or schedules. They did everything they could to not be absent, but when they had to miss school, they made up their work immediately.

The global students were quick to name much more social aspects of school as their favorites. Recess, lunch, and PE topped the list, but they also liked any class that included discussion, interaction, or group projects. Surprisingly, both globals and analytics often enjoyed math or science. The analytics liked the structure and black-and-white nature of those classes; the globals usually liked the subjects because they loved the teachers. When the globals missed school, their first question was usually, "Did I miss anything important?" They wanted to know if anything happened with their friends or schoolmates while they were gone. However, they were quick to add that they *did* care about the work they had missed.

The Homeschool Advantage

If you are homeschooling an analytic child, you'll find charts and lists and calendars will be very helpful in keeping everyone on track. Your analytic will count on sticking to a routine, and he or she may actually prefer to do worksheets rather than creative projects. Although that can make it easier for you to follow a prescribed curriculum, it may also be challenging if you are more global yourself. What seems like the inspiration of the moment to you may be a frustrating interruption to your child.

IN THEIR OWN WORDS

I think I'd learn better at school if it was just me and the teacher.

—Ariel, fourth grade

If you are homeschooling a more global child, you'll find he or she is probably much happier when spending time with you or other kids. Working alone is pretty unappealing, and you may find yourself having to constantly check on your child's progress to make sure there's no procrastination. If you are a more analytic parent, you can become frustrated with the apparent lack of concern about details, schedules, and deadlines. The upside is how cooperative your global can be when you plan field trips and creative projects.

STRETCHING THE SHOE

Some Practical and Immediate Adaptations

- Encourage your child to find a study partner who is the opposite style. Have them compare notes and after a while, try to listen in class through the eyes and ears of the other person.
- Help your child personalize deadline schedules; have her look at what the actual deadline is, decide what will realistically work, and reward herself for getting the final product done on time or even early.
- Add your own ideas:

____

____

____

CHANGING THE SHOE

Some Ideal Solutions

- Establish the 60-second rule: As long as you can retrieve what you need in 60 seconds or less, the organization system works. If you *can't* find it in that amount of time, keep refining the system until you can.
- Provide opportunities for teamwork—make sure each team member gets credit and takes responsibility for his own tasks while contributing to the whole effort.

- Add your own ideas:

____

____

____

PART 3

SURVIVING AND ADAPTING TO SCHOOL

11 WHO NEEDS HOMEWORK?

As in pressuring for homework, if we pressure students to learn what they do not want to learn, and then punish them with low grades when they do not learn it, they counter by taking schoolwork out of their quality worlds, and we lose them as learners.

—William Glasser, *The Quality School*

How often do you argue with your children about homework? How many evenings have ended in frustration, and how many times has everyone gone to bed irritated with each other? When was the last time you looked at that progress slip or report card and discovered that the low grade was a result of not doing the required homework?

It's certainly not a new issue—parents and kids have been battling over homework for generations. But now, more than ever, finding the time to do it and convincing students of the relevance of it presents a unique and sometimes insurmountable challenge. Many educators believe that homework should not even be assigned in the early elementary grades. After all, frequently kids don't get to spend any time just being kids. All day they have had to sit

IN THEIR OWN WORDS

I think I'd study better at home if I could keep the things at home and school separate. I have a life at home.

—Jennifer, seventh grade

in uncomfortable desks and listen to teachers and write notes and concentrate on learning. When that last school bell rings, most students can't wait to get out the door and head home. But what waits at home? Is it playtime and relaxation and conversation with family and friends? Not usually. It's time to hit the books again and try to finish as much homework as possible before dinner. When dinner's over, the work frequently goes on into the evening, and before you know it, it's time for bed. For highly active kids, their muscles are fairly screaming for physical activity, and bedtime can easily turn into a huge battle.

Although all kids can suffer, Dr. James Dobson points out that this situation is especially difficult for young children:

> I believe homework for young children can be counterproductive if not handled very, very carefully. Little kids are asked to sit for five or more hours per day doing formal class work. Then many of them take a tiring bus ride home. Then guess what? They're placed at a desk and told to do more assignments. For a wiry, active, fun-loving youngster, that's asking too much. Learning for them becomes an enormous bore instead of the exciting panorama that it ought to be.[12]

Many educators believe that homework should not be assigned at all during the elementary years. Others point out that some homework is valuable—reviewing for tests, memorizing the multiplication tables, studying spelling, reading for your book report. Most educators recognize that currently a lot of assigned homework is not achieving the desired result if the goal was to help students learn the concepts better and continue to master a particular subject. Instead, homework seems to frequently cause more stress, more boredom, and more lowered grades on a report card than any other single aspect of school.

Should all homework be banned? I am not one of those who insist there should be none at all. But I do believe that homework given just for the sake of keeping kids busy or given as a punishment does not justify having students dread learning or hate school. Most educators agree that homework should not be information that is new to the student; it should not be material there wasn't time to cover during class. It should, at the very least, be reinforcement of what has been taught, but in his book, *The Quality School,* William Glasser goes even further in his suggestion:

> A colleague of mine has suggested that homework should be work that can only be done at home rather than an extension of class work as most of it is now. For example, assignments in which students are asked to interview their parents, watch a specific program on educational television, do research in the community, volunteer for community service, practice at home or in the community what is learned in school. To promote creativity and initiative, an assignment might be to figure out what could be done at home that would enrich what is being studied in class.[13]

Dr. Mel Levine agrees, but he goes even further:

> The school should assign homework for parents. That homework should consist of activities parents can conduct with their children to reinforce what they are learning in school. Teachers can readily transmit such expectations through e-mail to all parents whose children are in their class. Who knows, moms and dads might even be able to update or upgrade their own knowledge and skills while helping their sons and daughters.[14]

Actually, for many parents, *that* kind of homework assignment would be a welcome relief from the last-minute, frantic race to help a child complete a project or finish a report. Sometimes parents don't even know what the point of the homework assignment is—they just know if their children don't do it, their grades usually suffer. The parents are often hard pressed to offer an acceptable explanation to their children for why homework must be done in the first place other than the tried-and-true "because you'll get a bad grade if you don't." The truth is, many teachers don't even really grade the homework assignments—they get checked off as having been completed and averaged into the overall grade. But if the point of the homework was just to accumulate scores in a grade book, it really doesn't seem worth it.

IN THEIR OWN WORDS

I think I'd study better at home if notes were provided on a teacher's web site.

—Travis, eighth grade

As educators and parents sort out the pros and cons of all this, homework is a reality most students and parents can't afford to ignore. So while we're trying to adjust this part of the educational system, let's look at some immediately useful and surprisingly practical ways to help everyone live with it.

Environmental Preferences

If your child is already uncomfortable learning in school, having to do homework in a space that closely resembles the traditional classroom may be the last thing she needs. Home is where you can experiment with factors that might not be adjustable anywhere else. Encourage your child to try various light, design, and temperature settings to see what helps her concentrate best. Allow at least a certain amount of eating and drinking whenever possible, and do your best to arrange the homework schedule around your child's best time of day. Remember to emphasize throughout the trial-and-error period that only what actually results in getting the homework done satisfactorily will be approved by you. Accountability should always stay intact.

Auditory Learners

A highly auditory learner usually needs to talk through the homework assignment in order to get a handle on what he's doing. If he can't talk to anyone about it, he may keep procrastinating until he gets that opportunity. He may find it hard to work with other people's noises, no matter how soft. Even the buzz in a light or the faraway sound of a car engine can sometimes be enough to distract him. On the other hand, he usually needs his own auditory noise in order to focus on the task at hand. You might try letting him wear headphones to drown out the rest of the world's sounds while he concentrates on his studying. Encourage him to find the background sounds that help him filter out distractions the best.

Visual Learners

At home, visual learners often enjoy having a visually appealing study space. Ideally, they'd like to have the cutting-edge computer desk, the latest in technology, the most contemporary school gear. Realistically, they can't have every cool-looking gadget they'd like, and even if they could it wouldn't necessarily increase the likelihood of getting the homework done. But visuals love bright colors and slick surfaces and up-to-date accessories. Challenge your visual child to find and furnish a study space within a specific budget. Remind her she must be able to prove that the expenditures will have the desired results.

Kinesthetic Learners

Studying at home is often torture for any active learner. He has had to be quiet and still in a classroom all day, and the thought of having to do it all evening is unbearable. He needs to blow off steam, let out energy, release some stress. If you do have to insist he does homework right away, at least let him take several short breaks during the time he's studying. There's no absolute rule that you have to work for an uninterrupted hour. Help your child look for ways to combine activity and study—pace or walk around while memorizing; walk up and down the stairs while reviewing for a test; shoot hoops in the driveway while going over math facts. The more your action-oriented learner can put action with what he's learning, the better the chances are that he will remember what he's studying!

Global Learners

For globals, one of the biggest challenges of homework is to simply realize you have it, write down what it is, and remember to take the right books home for it. The end of the school day brings with it a flurry of activity—going to your locker, touching base with lots of friends from other classes, getting on the bus. Making time to organize your books and binder so you're sure you have everything you need is a distant, if not non-existent, priority. I worked with one school that set aside the last ten minutes of every school day for every student to make sure that they knew what the evening's assignments were, they understood the directions for doing them, they had the books they would need, and they knew when everything was due. This was done each day by an announcement from the principal. All teaching ceased, and the readiness exercise began. The teachers were still there to provide clarification, study buddies could compare notes, and even the most global student could plan which books to take and which books to keep in his locker.

IN THEIR OWN WORDS

I think I'd study better at home if the work was more exciting.

—Chelsea, sixth grade

Once globals get home, one of the hardest things about studying is that you usually have to do it by yourself. When a global is alone, she can think of dozens of other activities she'd rather be doing—and all of them involve talking to someone else. She knows other members of her family are doing things that seem much more enjoyable. She is distracted by her mom or dad making dinner, her brother fixing his skateboard, or her neighbor mowing the lawn. Even if she's sitting at the desk with her book open, chances are good she's daydreaming about what she'd rather be doing. One of the best ways to help her focus and concentrate is to sit down and work *with* her. That doesn't mean you have to do the same work or even help her do hers—it just means you're not having any more fun than *she* is. She needs to read her book; you pick up a book and read too. She needs to do her math worksheet; you work on your shopping list.

IN THEIR OWN WORDS

Busy work creates enormous animosity.

—Jeremy, twelfth grade

Analytic Learners

Usually, the analytic student leaves school prepared to complete the necessary homework before he returns the next morning. He doesn't hesitate to ask his teacher for clarification, and often he tries to get a head start on the assignments before he even leaves school. He is eager to get home and just get the homework over with so he can have time to call his own. He has his own schedule in mind, and if he gets home to find his parents have made plans that prevent him from following his own format, he can become very annoyed.

He almost always works best in a clean, uncluttered space, even if it's in the middle of a chaotic, rumpled room.

The one spot where he is writing must be clear, and he needs to work without interruptions. It is often the global parent who breaks into his concentration several times with short directives: "When you're done, I need you to take out the trash." "As soon as you get to a good stopping place, I need you to help your sister." " Let me know when you're almost finished so I can set the table." Most analytics tell me that after the third such interruption, they might as well just give up getting *anything* done.

Virtually every analytic I've met prefers to be left alone while studying. They don't want to get together in a study group (after all, it sounds to them like it's a bunch of people who just want to suck the information out of the analytics who did all the work!). That doesn't mean they don't enjoy socializing; it just means they can't relax until the work's done. If you can help your analytic find the ideal place to concentrate where he will be alone and uninterrupted, you'll probably have very little trouble getting him to do the work.

What's the Point?

Even if students don't agree with the reason for doing their homework, they do deserve to know what that reason *is*. If you honestly don't know either, encourage your child to respectfully ask the teacher what the homework is supposed to accomplish so he or she will know if it's being done properly. As a parent, you may also have to ask the teacher to occasionally define the point so you can help your child understand the importance of doing the assignments. If either you or your child find yourselves having to guess what the point of the homework is, try answering these questions:

- Does it count toward the final grade? If so, how much?
- Will it reinforce the skills you'll need to perform well on the test?
- Will it help you learn more?
- Is it just a hoop you have to jump through in order to pass the class?

Is It Worth It?

I have to admit that when I was younger and I missed a day of school, I would often rather just take a zero on missed assignments and average it in than bother with the makeup work. My sister was just the opposite—she would call a friend from her sick bed and make arrangements to get the missed work before the day was over. Grades were very important to my sister, and she was meticulous about completing every assignment and doing her best on every test. I wasn't a bad student, but I felt like life was too short to focus so exclusively on school that I missed out on other activities and events. My sister ended up with straight A's throughout school, and continues to be very successful as an adult. I got A's in the classes I loved, and B's and C's in the ones I didn't like. I ended up with a B average overall, got my bachelor's degree, and finished a graduate degree a few years later.

You may have one child who is a high achiever and another who is content to simply get by. You may even have a child who doesn't want to work at all. You can't *make* any of your children want to do better—only they can decide to do that. If you never settled for less than top grades, it might really drive you crazy if you have a child who doesn't value A's like you did. If you were a B-average student, you might be concerned about your child who seems obsessed with getting top scores all the time. The bottom line is this—both you and your child have to answer a very important question: Is it worth it? If you have a perfectionist, chances are good you won't have to hover and remind him or her about doing homework. But if your child is resisting the whole idea of homework and keeps arguing that it doesn't matter anyway, both of you need to sit down and answer these questions:

- What grade do you want to get in this class?
- Realistically, how much homework could you skip and still get that grade?
- What happens if you get a lower grade?
- Will it really take that long to do this particular assignment?

What Will It Take?

If you have succeeded in getting your child to commit to the grade he or she really wants, now you're in a position to help design a plan for achieving the desired result. You may have had lots of good ideas before, but your child wasn't ready to buckle down and do anything because it wasn't his idea to change in the first place. You've asked and answered the two most important questions: What's the point? and Is it worth it? Now you and your child are ready for the action part: What will it take? Here are some good questions for starting your discussion and designing your plan of action:

- Do you want to be reminded of your homework? If so, how?

- When do you want to do your homework?
- What's the best environment for getting your homework done?
- What will you need to do your best work?

Points to Remember

If your children keep complaining that homework seems pointless and stupid, remind them of these important points:

- Beginning with your freshman year of high school, your grades will be recorded on your permanent record and will start counting toward the transcripts that factor into college and career decisions.
- No one else can do your homework for you. Even if your parents do your work or you bribe a friend or buy an assignment from the internet, you won't receive the benefits and your conscience will eventually drive you crazy. Only you can decide if it's worth it.
- Sometimes you just grit your teeth, take a deep breath, and get it over with.

If you're confident you can do well in the class and on the tests without doing the homework, be prepared to prove it. Give the teacher a written proposal, suggesting that if you achieve a particular score or higher on the test, you do not have to do any more homework than you feel is necessary. If you do not achieve that minimum score, you agree to go back and do the assigned homework you missed.

The Homeschool Advantage

When you are homeschooling, *all* schoolwork is homework! You have a unique opportunity to help your children figure out what works best when it comes to environment and learning style approach, but it's not always easy to accept what they tell you. Remember, accountability remains paramount when you begin to experiment with various ways to learn and remember. There's nothing magic about sitting in school desks and listening to a teacher lecture. If you know what the point is to what your child needs to learn, you'll be able to effectively communicate just about anything. One of my favorite Bible passages in Eugene Peterson's version, *The Message,* talks about homeschooling from the very beginning:

> Write these commandments that I've given you today on your hearts. Get them inside of you and then get them inside your children. Talk about them wherever you are, sitting at home or walking in the street; talk about them from the time you get up in the morning to when you fall into bed at night. Tie them on your hands and foreheads as a reminder; inscribe them on the doorposts of your homes and on your city gates. (Deuteronomy 6:6–9)

That sure sounds like a lot of flexibility without sacrificing bottom-line accountability—and you are just the ones to do it!

STRETCHING THE SHOE

Some Practical and Immediate Adaptations

- Encourage your child to use study buddies whenever possible so the more global students can stay on track and the more analytic students can have an opportunity to instruct and direct.

- Personalize your child's schedule and work time so that globals can work more flexibly and with others and analytics can have more time and space alone. Allow for frequent breaks if they are needed.
- Add your own ideas:

____

____

____

CHANGING THE SHOE

Some Ideal Solutions

- Clearly identify the purpose of homework—and make almost all homework interactive with parents or applicable to outside community activities or interests.
- Design an individual study space for each child according to what helps him or her concentrate and focus best.
- Add your own ideas:

____

____

____

____

What Are We Testing?

I know some kids who ought to exercise a right not to have their intelligence tested. They run the high risk of having their minds misrepresented by a score.

—Mel Levine, M.D., *A Mind at a Time*

The definition is on the blackboard, but Jeff doesn't write it down. After all, he doesn't know what it means. He's waiting for the teacher to say that magic phrase: "In other words . . ." And then the light comes on in Jeff's head and the concept becomes clear and he gets it. Until the test. What's on the test? Well, that would be the definition Jeff didn't write down. In fact, he doesn't recognize *half* the information asked for on the test. When did they talk about *that?* He thought he *knew* this! Jeff gets that sinking feeling again. How can a kid understand this stuff so well and get such crummy grades on the test?

Unfortunately, Jeff's global learning style is at odds with his teacher's analytic testing style. Although his big-picture mind grasps concepts and ideas quickly, it doesn't naturally break down the information into specific parts or focus on the details. And Jeff, as bright as he is, looks like he either didn't study or didn't pay attention.

Robert is one of our very active sons, and he was the first preschooler in his class to memorize "The Pledge of Allegiance." We had some guests over, and I asked Rob if he'd like to tell us his pledge. His chest puffed out with pride as he nodded. Quickly he began to walk away as we faintly heard the first few words of his recitation. "Robert," I said, "we can't hear you when you walk away. Come stand in front of these nice people and tell them your pledge." I practically had to wrestle him into position and hold him with all my strength to get him to stand still and face his audience. But he stood in silence. He couldn't even think of the first word—until I let him go. As soon as he could walk and talk, he could remember everything. As long as Rob is on the move, his mind works like a well-oiled machine. Make him sit still—and nothing. The information is either stuck, or it leaked out. But he can't remember a thing.

Unfortunately, from the time our school system began, there has been one primary method of making sure students can prove they know what they were taught. They have to take a test. Think about it for a moment. Can you move around during most tests? The kinesthetic student can answer that: No. Can you verbalize your thoughts during most tests? The auditory student can answer that: No. Can you perhaps bring in a drawing or two on your hand to help you visualize the answer on a test? The visual student can answer that: No. If the only way you ever test students for what they know is to sit them down in a quiet, still environment, give them paper and pencil, start the timer, and make sure they don't move until they're finished, it's not surprising that so many kids—including the grownup one writing this book—have never shown how much they know. Many of us know ten times more than we are ever able to demonstrate on a typical test. As adults, we can prove it by using our intuitive, entrepreneurial, creative instincts. But there aren't many tests in school that measure those things.

I know what some of you might be thinking—I'm advocating not giving tests to students at all. But that's not it. Let's just not get confused between tests and accountability. Accountability should never be sacrificed. Sometimes a paper-and-pencil test is the best form of accountability. Sometimes it's the worst. The most important question to ask is a familiar one: What's the point? If we are clear about what our tests are measuring, we might be surprised to find how many ways there are to measure the same outcome. Dr. Mel Levine has developed "a school for all kinds of minds." Here's how he describes his testing philosophy:

IN THEIR OWN WORDS

Something I don't think I'll ever need to know again after I get out of school is science. I mean, does it really matter in the world if we know the parts of a flower and a worm?

—Robbie, seventh grade

> I believe all kids should have a strong base of knowledge across a wide range of subject areas. Every citizen should be culturally and scientifically literate. But we should be offering much wider curriculum choices, particularly in secondary schools. Every student should

> undergo some form of competency assessment. But is it fair to test them all the same way on the same material? In our school for all kinds of minds students would have some choice in what they wanted to be evaluated in and how they wanted to be evaluated.[15]

I'm not talking about leveling the playing field or letting students off with the excuse that a test will hurt their self-esteem. I'm talking about finding the best way to measure the level of knowledge and competency in a student—and that's almost impossible to do when you insist the student take the kind of test in the kind of circumstances that work against their individual style. That doesn't mean students shouldn't learn to take all kinds of tests—I believe they need that kind of discipline. But when the testing process becomes so rigid and so narrow that only a very few kinds of tests determine the most critical outcomes for all kinds of students, something is fundamentally wrong with the system.

To me, a classic example of not defining what we measure is the timed math test that plagues virtually every first and second grade student. I struggled with this, because we have twin boys, in separate classes, and during their first and second grade years, the timed tests were a real sore spot with me. Mike, our more analytic son, whipped right through those problems, finishing with time to spare. Robert, the global, got every problem right, but somehow the "tick, tick, tick, ding!" of the timer distracted him so much he had a hard time finishing the required number of equations. The tests were scaled from "A" to "Z" in increasing difficulty, and Mike took great pleasure in pointing out to his brother that he was significantly ahead of him, so that must mean Mike was smarter. We did a lot of coaching, reminding both boys that their strengths were not identical, but their intelligence was equally high. I talked to both teachers and the principal, trying to determine what the purpose of the tightly controlled timed exercises was. After some discussion, we got to the core of the matter. The children need to become adept at quickly adding sums so that when they begin to do multiplication, the ability to do quick addition is just second nature. The explanation, of course, makes sense, and I have no argument with that outcome. I did, however, propose an alternative. Why couldn't the students write down the time when they started their test, write down the time when they finished, and then consistently try to beat their own best time? No "tick, tick, tick, ding!" There is still accountability, and the standard is not lowered—but there's also another road to the same destination. So far, my alternative has not been embraced with enthusiasm, but it takes a while to change a practice that's been in place for a couple hundred years!

IN THEIR OWN WORDS

The thing I don't understand about school is how grades are what determine what you've learned. I can pass every test with A's and B's, but fail the class because of my homework grades. I don't think I learn from homework. My grades never show what I learned.

—Danny, high school student

Tests will always be a part of academic life at every level of education. Even if all teachers everywhere decided not to give classroom tests, we would still need to deal with standardized tests, intelligence tests, entrance exams, and so forth. While we are working to make the tests themselves better, let's take a look at some coping strategies for different learning styles that can help increase the likelihood of student success in the meantime.

For Auditory Learners

For most auditory students, one of the biggest challenges of taking tests is that you have to be so quiet. The whole room is quiet, and any whispering or mumbling automatically makes you a suspect for cheating. You certainly can't make any "thinking noises," so your ears are often hypersensitive to the humming in the light fixtures or heat vents, the sounds of students swallowing, and a dozen other potentially distracting sounds. You can't talk your way through your thought process—at least not out loud—yet you often need to talk to yourself as you go.

Something that may work for auditory learners is to practice working or taking tests in silent places. You might even want to make a game of it, having someone actually try to distract you with progressively louder noises and see how much you can handle before the distraction becomes too great. Believe it or not, with time and practice you can condition your auditory brain to tune those noises out. Even if teachers do their best to accommodate your learning style when taking classroom tests, you'll need to be able to survive the formally administered standardized tests given for college entrance and other purposes.

In class, some teachers will allow highly auditory students to wear headphones while taking the test in order to drown out distracting noises. The teacher, of course, decides what is playing in the headphones—and sometimes it's nothing at all. There are usually not that many students who truly need this adjustment, but those who do tell us it really makes a significant difference.

In extreme cases, teachers will sometimes offer to give auditory students the test verbally, letting the students tell them the answers as they read the questions. Usually, this is done only after the students have taken their best shot at the standard test without success. Often, when students know they have the safety net of being able to talk out the test if they fail, they actually relax and do okay on the test after all.

Visual Learners

One of the biggest challenges for the visual learners is not being distracted by the appearance of the test itself. Depending on the format, some tests can look overwhelming and formidable just by virtue of the bubbles, the length of the questions, or the number of choices. Teachers who make an effort to allow more white space, type in bigger print, and minimize the amount of information on any one page frequently find more students who do not feel threatened by the look of the test itself.

There are a few books on test-taking strategies that, in my opinion, are not only practical but are very compatible with different learning styles. *Test-Taking Strategies* by Judi Kesselman-Turkel and Franklynn Peterson and several age-appropriate volumes by Gary Gruber are my timeless standbys. One of my all-time favorite test tips is especially good for visual and global learners like me. On a multiple-choice test, all the answers except the right one are officially called "distracters." That's a very accurate depiction, since I can easily be led astray by the choices. Here's what often works: I cover all the answer options with my hand and read the question. In my head, I decide what the right answer is before I lift my hand and look at the choices. I quickly choose the one that most closely resembles the answer in my head, mark it, and move on to the next question. Now this won't help if you haven't studied—but if you know the information, you'll be surprised how this technique can help you focus.

Kinesthetic Learners

It's not hard to figure out why highly kinesthetic learners have trouble concentrating during a traditional test. Most testing situations demand you sit still for a long period of time, and any restlessness on your part can create suspicion in the mind of the test-giver. You aren't given any breaks until the test is completely over, and the active mind and body of the kinesthetic kid may find itself so distracted it can block the memory.

Sometimes something as simple as a piece of clay or a soft stress ball held and manipulated by the student during the test can overcome a lot of the discomfort caused by inactivity. Some studies have claimed that chewing gum not only lets the student move something while working, but the chewing can actually increase brain wave activity. The jury's still out on that—you can see what kind of complications could arise!

As with the auditory learner, the kinesthetic child can also benefit by "practicing" the testing situation. Challenge these kids not only to be able to stay still longer, but also to find ways they can use acceptable movement—highlighting, doodling, and so on.

Analytic Learners

Most analytic students tell me they don't really mind most tests. They see it as a challenge to be met, and they definitely want the opportunity to get the highest score in the class. Objective tests are their favorites, because the black-and-white, right-or-wrong nature of the questions leaves no room for vague generalities. Most analytics have kept track during class of what will be on the test, and if there are any surprises, the teacher will likely be bombarded with critical questions and arguments for adjusting the score.

If an analytic suffers from test anxiety, sometimes the best thing to do is to help him learn to pace himself and figure out which parts of the test count most. If the test is written by a more global teacher, it may be difficult for the analytic student to figure out exactly what kind of answer the teacher wants. A practice quiz or two before the big test can help the analytic figure out the teacher's testing style and anticipate what kind of questions will be on the test that really count.

Global Learners

Although analytic learners like objective tests best, globals usually like them the least. It's so hard to reduce everything you know into sterile, quick, black-and-white responses. I've had several global students over the years that took an extremely long time to take a simple twenty-five-item true-false test because beside each answer they had to explain *why* they said true or *why* they said false. Globals much prefer essay questions—that way, they can write a whole lot of stuff about a whole lot of things and hopefully the teacher will find the right answer in there somewhere. It's not hard to figure out why analytic teachers are not fond of that kind of test!

Most globals take tests much more personally than their analytic counterparts do. The globals are sure the test is designed to make them look dumb or feel like a failure. Every item could be a trick question, and the globals can second-guess themselves into a failing grade even when they know the information very well. One of the most effective strategies for globals sounds pretty minor, but it has surprisingly positive results: dress comfortably and don't come hungry. Globals are very tuned in to class atmosphere and team efforts, and the more relaxed they feel about their surroundings, the less they feel threatened by the test.

The Homeschool Advantage

When you teach your children at home, you don't have to use typical tests or even those given to you in the prescribed curriculum workbooks. You can challenge your child to show his knowledge in ways other than paper-and-pencil tests, always being clear about what outcomes you need to have demonstrated. Even children who prefer the relative security of the familiar forms of testing should be encouraged to occasionally step out and try an untraditional approach. By the same token, your children who struggle with testing should practice getting good enough at the standard methods to at least survive the tests they will be required to take outside your home.

In the end, you'll find that asking and answering the question "What's the point?" will still provide your best tool for helping your children master the knowledge they need.

STRETCHING THE SHOE

Some Practical and Immediate Adaptations

- Encourage your child to let the teacher know how uncomfortable he is with the testing process. Ask for tips on how to take the kind of tests the teacher usually gives.
- Once you get to know how a particular teacher tests, suggest that your child try to think about the test questions as the teacher teaches the material in the first place. Have her check with her study buddy and compare notes—try to anticipate what items are most likely to show up on the test.
- Add your own ideas:

____

____

____

CHANGING THE SHOE

Some Ideal Solutions

- Provide alternatives to paper-and-pencil tests that still demonstrate that the student knows the same information the test was supposed to measure—projects, discussions, and so forth.

- For those students who particularly dread the formal test process, offer a second chance—if the student takes the test and feels he or she just froze or failed because of the actual process, they can arrange to retake the test the same day, with the teacher or designated aide letting them verbally give their answers.

- Add your own ideas:

____

____

____

13 Getting Along with Your Teachers

Students will do things for a teacher they care for that they would not consider doing for a teacher they did not care for.

—William Glasser, *The Quality School*

Mrs. Rogers is on her way to the 3:30 faculty meeting. It's 3:28, and just before she walks into the cafeteria where the meeting is being held, a distraught student intercepts her and asks for help. Mrs. Rogers smiles sympathetically and tells the student she has a meeting but it shouldn't be long. If he'll wait either here in the hall or in her room, she'll sit down with him and help him work this problem out before she leaves for the day. At 3:29, she makes a timely entry into the faculty meeting.

Mr. Parker is on his way to the 3:30 faculty meeting. It's 3:28, and just before he walks into the cafeteria where the meeting is being held, a distraught student intercepts him and asks for help. Mr. Parker smiles sympathetically and draws the student down the hall to his room. They spend some time talking through the student's problem and coming up with workable solutions before the student goes home, smiling and relieved. At 4:45, Mr. Parker has missed the entire faculty meeting.

Which of these teachers cares more for the distraught student? The answer, of course, is that they both care very much. But Mrs. Rogers and Mr. Parker, both fine teachers, are very different in style and approach. Mrs. Rogers is more analytic, and she puts a high priority on scheduled commitments and tasks completed on time. Mr. Parker is more global, and people and the "teachable moment" will almost always take priority over schedules and timelines. He will make sure he gets the information from the faculty meeting, but he simply could not ask the student to wait until the business was out of the way.

Education is one of the fields that really lends itself to all kinds of learning styles. There are good teachers who can teach students who learn like they do, or students who are almost exactly opposite. Most students will tell you that it isn't usually the style of the teacher that makes the most difference—it's the relationship the teacher has with individual students. If students feel valued and respected by their teachers, even boring lectures or difficult assignments are easier to take.

For the purposes of this book, I'm going to talk in terms of good teachers, since I believe that by far there are more good teachers than poor ones. Most teachers would do a lot more to identify and teach to individual student learning styles if they had the freedom to do so. But many teachers are burdened with overwhelming tasks, and without support from administrators, school boards, and the school system as a whole, teachers face an uphill climb when it comes to integrating learning styles into their daily routines and curriculum. There are some teachers, both in public and private schools, that should not be teaching—but it is not my purpose here to deal with that aspect. We will focus on the most positive ways possible for helping students and teachers alike learn to use their strengths to help every child succeed.

No teacher is only one learning style any more than any student is just one style. Everyone is a mix, with several pieces influencing how they teach and learn. It's also important to note that how a student perceives her teacher's style depends, to a great extent, on what the student's *own* style is. I have gone into many classrooms to teach learning styles, and when I ask the class as a whole what style they think their teacher is, I've never gotten a unanimous answer.

IN THEIR OWN WORDS

I think I'd learn better at school if I was the only one in school because if I was raising my hand she would answer my question and then go on.

—Alison, fourth grade

There are those who suggest students should always be matched with teachers who share their dominant learning style preferences. Although that may be a good idea in the primary grades, I don't believe it's always the best plan as a child gets older. Part of any student's education should be learning to have the ability to get along with a variety of learning styles—whether they're your parent, your teacher, or your boss. It's a big, diverse world out there, and we have to learn to work and live in lots of circumstances. But remember, awareness is half the battle, and learning to recognize why one teacher can be so effective with certain students and not with others or why some students do so well in some classes and not in others, can make a big difference when it comes to succeeding in school *and* in life.

It shouldn't surprise you that teachers tend to use teaching methods that work for *them*. Even though teacher education classes do a good job of training student teachers to believe and practice certain uniform techniques and methods, it's impossible to remove an individual's influence on how he or she teaches. Researcher Walter Barbe points out: "As adults, we structure our environment according to our modality. This is also true of teachers and their classrooms. Teachers teach the way they learn best."[16] Although there are exceptions, you can definitely recognize learning style patterns when you observe most teachers in action.

Auditory Teachers

A teacher who is more auditory usually requires students to talk more—not only with respect to discussions and answering questions, but also in daily interactions. You hear them saying things like: "All right, everyone repeat after me" or "Let's all say this together" or "Turn to your neighbor and tell them . . ." For the auditory students, this is not a problem, but for other styles, the constant demands to use their verbal skills can be a little frustrating. Although the auditory teacher may talk a lot, she sometimes insists that the classroom stay quiet, and will be much less tolerant of student interruptions (after all, she can't think with someone else's noise!). If students are really listening, however, they will almost always know what their teacher is thinking and planning!

Visual Teachers

A visual teacher usually makes use of lots of handouts, and relies on charts, diagrams, and posters. Visual students may actually become distracted more easily, since their teacher probably furnishes the classroom with brightly colored and visually stimulating objects. The visual teacher may not talk as freely, either to the class in general or to the students individually. Chances are better that this teacher uses a lot more silent observation in class, and communicates more readily by writing notes or drawing pictures. Remember, no teacher will *just* be visual; there will usually be either an auditory or kinesthetic backup style. If you are more frequently asked to turn in written assignments than to participate in verbal discussions, you'll be getting a pretty strong clue about your teacher's dominant modality.

Kinesthetic Teachers

You could probably guess how to spot a more kinesthetic teacher—although you'll have to keep moving to find them! Kinesthetic students have to constantly force themselves to sit still and pay attention, but kinesthetic teachers have the advantage of being able to wander around the classroom and stay active. If your teacher has this as his dominant modality, you won't find him at his desk very often. He may consistently circle the classroom while students are working, and he probably doesn't have many assignments that involve long periods of working in one place. In the upper grades, highly kinesthetic teachers are often hired as coaches, due to their strengths in the area of movement and agility. Ironically, the principal may become frustrated when these same coaches and teachers won't sit through a long faculty meeting!

Analytic Teachers

Most analytic teachers keep their classrooms as organized as their lesson plan book. Although there may be charts and diagrams and fire drill instructions, there usually will not be much in the way of "homey" atmosphere builders. These teachers want their students to focus on the information being taught, and often believe that too much in the way of visual stimulation will simply distract from the goal. Analytic teachers will let you know right up front what their requirements are and what the consequences will be for infractions. You'll usually receive a syllabus in the upper grades, and a neat list of rules and instructions in the elementary grades. You can almost always count on having a seating chart, and the teacher will make a concerted effort to keep every student individually accountable for his or her work and behavior. Chances are good there won't be many group projects or discussions, as the analytic wants to make sure independent work is recognized and rewarded. The grading scale will be clearly

IN THEIR OWN WORDS

I don't even care about desks, classroom temperatures, or the time of day when the teacher is qualified, intelligent, organized, *and* creative.

—Rachelle, twelfth grade

outlined, and strictly adhered to, in most cases. If 92–100 is an A, then a 91.4 is a B. They believe that student self-esteem is important, but are convinced that the best way to gain that self-esteem is by experiencing success, especially in difficult situations. Their standards are high, and if they seem to be harder on their students than their more global colleagues, it's just because they want them to go out into the world stronger and smarter.

The Global Teachers

Global teachers, as a rule, don't look nearly as organized in outward appearance as analytic teachers do. The global teacher has lots of piles waiting to be filed, and is constantly searching for materials that would help inspire and encourage students to appreciate and love what they're learning. The classroom is often designed as a "home away from home" with rugs, pictures, plants, and other personal touches. Rather than provide a written outline of rules and grading guidelines, global teachers are much more likely to talk about general principles and deal with specific situations as they come up. They may start the year with seating charts, but they are usually flexible enough to let students do some rearranging as the semester progresses. There probably won't be nearly as many written assignments as there are class discussions and group projects. The all-for-one-one-for-all attitude is an important philosophy to globals, and these teachers try to discourage confrontational types of competition. The grading scale may be uniform, but if 92–100 is an A and a student who has been working very hard gets a 91.2, the chances are better than not that this student will still get an A. The global teachers believe student self-esteem is very important, and they may choose to spend a few days on lessons that help teach students about the subject. They don't let their students compromise basic standards, but they view themselves as coaches and facilitators who will send their kids into the world full of confidence in their ability and love for humankind.

Each style of teacher can contribute a great deal to a student's success. The key in achieving that success is often how well the student understands what the teacher is asking her to do, and how positive the relationship is that exists between the two. No one learning style makes a better teacher—all styles can be equally effective. But there's no question that sometimes an extreme mismatch between certain teacher and student styles can create more trouble than it's worth. I believe it's best for both the teacher and the students to identify their learning style strengths from the very beginning, knowing they will both have to do some stretching and accommodating. In situations where the differences are so great it becomes counterproductive for either the teacher or the student, certain measures must be taken to work out the best solution for all involved.

IN THEIR OWN WORDS

To make school more interesting, we need to do more hands-on activities or leave the school once in a while. We need to change the routine and not stare at the teacher in the front of the class all the time.

—Jeremiah, twelfth grade

The Homeschool Advantage

When you homeschool your children, you're both the parent *and* the teacher. This has an upside and a downside. The upside, of course, is that you know your child better than any teacher ever could. You understand the strengths, the limitations, and the frustrations, and you can adjust your teaching methods accordingly. The downside is that sometimes you blur the lines between being a parent and being a teacher, and there can be hard feelings carried over from interactions between you and your child on either side of the line. Both you and your children can get irritable and touchy after spending days and nights together, and it can become difficult to get the respect you need when you slide into your teacher mode.

One homeschool mom decided she would let her kids help her choose a "teacher hat." The hat would be a symbol of her deliberate change in role from being mom to being teacher. Although she did not have to wear the hat all the time she was in her teaching role, it was a clear signal when she wanted to begin her lessons. Her kids had a great time deciding on exactly which hat would be best, and it didn't take long for everyone to instantly recognize when it was time to start paying attention to the teacher.

STRETCHING THE SHOE

Some Practical and Immediate Adaptations

- Using the Teacher Profile Summary on pages 141–44, identify the primary differences between your child and the teacher—figure out why there might be conflicts that result in misunderstandings that aren't deliberate with either one of them.

- Help your children do their best to appreciate their teachers—even the most difficult ones are teaching them to get along with the world. Suggest they drop a note of appreciation to the teacher who irritates them most and give an honest word or two of praise. You *and* your children may be amazed at how much the relationship will improve with even a minimum amount of effort.

- Add your own ideas:

____

____

____

CHANGING THE SHOE

Some Ideal Solutions

- Every classroom could benefit by having team teachers, each of them an opposite dominant learning style. Not only would different teachers be more effective with different students, but *all* the students would have the opportunity to see style diversity and understand the value of opposite perspectives.
- Each teacher could greatly enhance relationships with students by an honest attitude of self-revelation. Let students know what your personal learning style strengths are, and what is likely to please or frustrate you. Outline your expectations, but explain that your own personal perspectives are bound to sometimes be misunderstood.

- Add your own ideas:

____

____

____

TEACHER PROFILE SUMMARY

It's important to remind your child that every teacher will have his or her individual learning style strengths and preferences too. It's natural for a teacher to insist students use methods that make sense to the teacher's own style. Usually, teachers are willing to be at least a little flexible, but occasionally there will be one who simply won't compromise. It's often a very beneficial thing to combine students and teachers with different and even opposite learning styles. The most important element of this, however, is an awareness on the part of the student regarding why the teacher's style can be so frustrating or difficult to understand. The following profile can help your child discover and understand some of the most obvious learning style differences of his or her teachers. If your child is too young to fill it out alone, fill out the profile as you discuss it with him.

TEACHER PROFILE SUMMARY

Student Name ______________________________

Date ________ Dominant Style ____________________

Teacher's Name ______________________________

Grade/Subject Taught ________________________

Place a check mark by all those that apply

1. How would you describe this teacher's room?

___looks organized
___has maps, charts, graphs
___feels like school
___predictable seating
___cool, calm colors

___looks disorganized
___has posters, plants, decorations
___feels more like home
___seating arrangement changes
___warm, cozy colors

2. How do you know about this teacher's rules?

___rules handed out in writing
___specific rules stated

___rules given as needed
___general guidelines given

3. What activities/teaching methods does this teacher use most often?

___lecture	___class discussion
___individual assignments	___group work
___step-by-step instructions	___overview of material
___written reports	___oral reports
___definite deadlines	___flexible deadlines
___gives objective examples	___shares lots of personal stories

4. What determines your grade most often?

___daily work	___extra credit
___tests/quizzes	___class participation
___attendance/tardies	___citizenship
___individual projects	___group projects
___how well you performed	___how hard you tried

5. How do you know this teacher respects or appreciates you?

___puts it in writing	___tells me personally
___calls on me in class	___hugs me, pats me on the back
___lets me be in charge	___praises me in front of everyone
___asks me what I think	___gives parties or extra recesses
___lets me work by myself	___lets me work with a partner
___doesn't let me know directly	___uses stickers, smiley faces, stars

6. **What style does this teacher seem to use most often? (add total check marks in columns)**

___Analytic ___Global

7. **How does this teacher's style make it easier for you to learn?**

____

____

8. **How does this teacher's style make it harder for you to learn?**

____

____

14 Redefining Diversity

Your child wants you to think of him and think "possibility," not deficiency. You may not approve of the things he does, but he needs your approval of him as a person. Your child's innate way of thinking is an intrinsic part of him. To him, it's the only style of thinking he's ever known. He yearns for you to accept him and to see in him a trait that says strength, not weakness.

—Lucy Jo Palladino, *The Edison Trait*

I spent six years as a fully commissioned reserve police officer. During that time, my fellow officers and I were required to attend several different training seminars about "cultural diversity" and "gender sensitivity." Sadly, most of the time, my colleagues and I left feeling more paranoid than ever. We almost dreaded meeting anyone who was not like us—what if we said the wrong thing? What if we failed to do the *right* thing? Rolling up to the scene of a crime, instead of first of all thinking of issues of life and death, we were often worried about liability and political correctness.

I believe we were being asked to focus on the wrong thing. The whole concept of learning styles transcends race, creed, color, gender, politics, and religion. Focusing on learning style strengths allows us to value each person for who he is as an individual before we look at any of the other pieces of the puzzle. Before you look at me as a Caucasian female CEO in the workplace, I want you to see the strengths I bring to the table. Look at my kinesthetic energy, my global intuitive creativity, my independent thinking. The other pieces of my puzzle are important, but I want to be valued most for who I am.

IN THEIR OWN WORDS

I'd do better in school if we could leave school and experience real life once in a while.

—Josh, high school student

We often struggle in our schools to help certain groups of disadvantaged students learn more effectively. We offer special programs for those children whom we term "at risk" for a number of critical reasons. We face unique challenges in many urban and inner-city school districts and in lower socioeconomic areas. For decades we have searched for the right balance when it comes to achieving an effective mix of ethnic and cultural backgrounds in any one school. We have pondered how much we should try to match teachers and students of similar race, religion, and gender. There is much controversy over studies that attempt to prove certain populations of students are either hampered or benefited simply by virtue of where they were born or how much money their parents have. Although these factors can play an important part in understanding why a particular program or approach may be effective, we are still focusing on the wrong primary goal.

If our goal is to help every child succeed—and I believe it should be—then we must go beyond the external issues of what children look like and where they are from. We must help each and every child discover his or her own natural learning strengths and use those strengths to overcome limitations and achieve success—even if those strengths are at odds with what the traditional classroom demands. One of the most consistent findings in learning style research is the fact that an individual's learning style is not dependent upon her IQ score. We are also slowly documenting the fact that a person's IQ score means very little when it comes to measuring a student's potential to achieve success anyplace other than the traditional classroom setting.

Howard Gardner's research on multiple intelligences has helped us discover how limited our measurement of intelligence has been, since there are several types of intelligence we don't recognize or value in our society or educational system. Dr. Gardner puts it this way:

> Most people in our society, even if they know better, talk as if individuals could be assessed in terms of one dimension, namely how smart or dumb they are. This is deeply ingrained in us. I became convinced some time ago that such a narrow assessment was wrong in scientific terms and had seriously damaging social consequences.[17]

Dr. Gardner's work around the world has shown how much true diversity there is, not only in terms of cultural factors, but also in terms of which of our areas of intelligence are valued in which society. Although our American society places a high value on a student's verbal and mathematical skills, a child growing up on a South Seas island may find his spatial abilities that enable him to navigate uncharted waters are much more valued. We in America have an incredible mix of cultures, often in the same classroom. To insist that one or two particular kinds of intelligence are the only measure of how smart or capable a child can be is truly doing an injustice to all of us. Again, I'm not talking about changing outcomes and performance or lowering any academic standards. I'm talking about finding the unique, inborn strengths in each child and helping that individual figure out how to apply those strengths to the challenge of learning.

IN THEIR OWN WORDS

I'm the kind of person that loves the social scene. If I don't have a lot of socializing throughout the day, I get really depressed.

—Desirae, high school student

Besides the cultural differences, there are times when gender can become a critical issue. A key example of this is in intelligence testing. Thomas Armstrong, in his book *In Their Own Way,* takes issue with the whole concept of "normal." He points out that the more we know about learning styles, the more we realize there's really no such thing as a "normal" child. In our efforts to define "normal" through intelligence testing, we've developed some artificial standards and created some misunderstandings between the genders.

> When IQ tests were first being developed, it turned out that girls consistently scored higher than boys on many of the items. In order to make things equal, testers threw out

> items that favored girls until a normal bell curve was attained for all children. Dian McGuinness, a University of South Florida psychologist, says that there are basic neuropsychological differences between the sexes.... She suggests that if the test takers took these gender differences into account when constructing their assessments—instead of making the data conform to some statistical ideal—"overnight millions of disabled boys would become normal readers" and many boys labeled as ADHD would be seen as displaying gender-appropriate traits.
>
> ... Who is to say that one child's blend of abilities/disabilities is any more or less normal than another child's?[18]

The bottom line is, where we were born, what gender we are, how we were reared—all of these issues are important pieces to our individual puzzles, and they have an effect on how we perceive and deal with the world. But none of these pieces should be used to label us when it comes to opportunities for learning. Whether we are a man or a woman, whether we grew up in the inner city or on a farm, whether we have a particular color of skin or accent in our speech—learning styles cut across all lines.

I have been saying this for years, but recently I got to put my theory into practice. I spent a week in the Caribbean, teaching young missionaries and speaking to a large group of youth workers from two different islands. In my missionary class, I was the only American; at the youth workers seminar, there were maybe two or three others, but almost everyone else was native to the area. I travel overseas at least once a year, but I'm always amazed to see how welcome this message is around the world. At the end of the Saturday seminar for area youth workers, a native woman rushed up to the front to speak to me. She was as short as I am tall; she was as dark as I am fair; she was as white-haired as I am not—but she threw her arms around me and exclaimed, "You're just like me!" And she was right. The more we talked, the more we discovered our minds worked in very similar ways, and we shared so many learning style puzzle pieces.

Regardless of race, creed, color, culture, religion, or politics, God made each of us to be a fearfully, wonderfully, complexly made individual. It's why we can turn to a perfect stranger and honestly say, "I like your style!"

The Homeschool Advantage

Depending on where you live, you may find yourself with limited opportunities to introduce your children to diverse cultural opportunities. Do your best to search out ways to learn and discuss contributions from many different cultures and various ethnic backgrounds. Focus on the similarities when it comes to learning styles, and try to identify how other countries may use the same learning styles we have, but in very different ways. Help your children practice finding the best in others by looking for how their learning style can contribute positively in a given situation.

STRETCHING THE SHOE

Some Practical and Immediate Adaptations

- Encourage your child to use an accountability partner to help him keep from demonstrating any talk or actions that could be interpreted as negative to someone who is unlike him. Suggest he and his partner have a code word they can use in order to draw each other's attention to the matter right away.

- Suggest your child look for ways she can identify learning styles in people all across the world; discuss the strengths of each style and what it can contribute to the given situation.
- Add your own ideas:

____

____

____

CHANGING THE SHOE

Some Ideal Solutions

- Find positive, productive ways to showcase learning style strengths, regardless of background or ethnicity.
- Provide opportunities for teamwork, making sure team members are different learning styles. Be sure the team members are aware of the style differences and similarities so they can take advantage of opposite talents and abilities.
- Add your own ideas:

____

____

____

PART 4

CHANGING THE SCHOOL, NOT YOUR CHILD

15 Why You May Not Want to Be "School Material"

Could it be that to a degree, our mind-set and educational format have outlived their usefulness? Every day we expect children to adapt to our way of thinking. Is it time to update our thinking and be more open to the potential of theirs?

—Lucy Jo Palladino, *The Edison Trait*

His name was David Neely,[19] and although he was only in the second grade, his file in the school office was almost three inches thick. Among other things, the reports in the file claimed David had Attention Deficit Hyperactivity Disorder (ADHD), Oppositional Defiant Disorder (ODD), dyslexia, and auditory processing problems. There were claims that David needed some anger management intervention and counseling for social interaction. At least one form was a referral for special education classes, and another form was waiting for a signature to allow David to apply for after-school care due to his being in a single-parent, dysfunctional family. David was only eight years old, but his file had already outgrown its original jacket. David's mother brought him to a professional counselor who, at the time, had an office just down the hall from ours. The counselor had a copy of David's file on her desk when she called the school psychologist at his elementary school.

"I have a copy of David Neely's file here," she told the psychologist, "and I see how many problem areas there are. But I was wondering—could you tell me some of David Neely's strengths?" The response from the school psychologist was honest, but surprising. "Oh, I'm sorry," he replied, "but we're not really set up to assess *strengths.*"

If you think about it, that's absolutely true. Our educational system has never been set up in a way that identifies student strengths. We know how to diagnose areas of weakness and set up programs to "fix" them, but we've never really done much when it comes to discovering and using individual student *strengths*. Of course, if that *did* happen, it would uncover a multitude of inconveniences for teachers, administrators, and the educational system in general. In her book *The Edison Trait,* Lucy Jo Palladino makes this point by using Thomas Edison as an example:

> As a child, Thomas Edison was a misfit in the classroom. His mind was constantly wandering and he couldn't sit still in his seat. He required personalized instruction. He needed to learn in his own style and at his own pace. Only then could he get himself on track, and turn his wild ideas and mischief into brilliance and scientific discovery.[20]

Some of the world's greatest thinkers, inventors, and innovators were in many ways the most inconvenient students. Can you think of any truly great men or women who never challenged the standard school system or thought "outside the box"? And yet, more today than ever, we keep expanding the definition of learning disorders and the parameters of special education to include almost any behavior that makes teaching or parenting the child more difficult. I believe there are very legitimate learning disorders and neurological and physiological disabilities. But I am also convinced we have gone entirely too far in our attempts to give almost any nonconforming or inconvenient behavior in our children a label that indicates there is something inherently *wrong* with the child.

By far the most dramatic example of this is the rapidly expanding diagnosis and treatment of Attention Deficit Hyperactivity Disorder (ADHD) or Attention Deficit Disorder (ADD). Although even the most prominent researchers and professionals in the field cannot agree on the symptoms, the cause, or the treatment, ADHD is one of the most commonly diagnosed conditions when parents and educators are looking for reasons students aren't doing better in the classroom. Dr. Peter Breggin, author of *Talking Back to Ritalin*, shares some startling facts:

> Recent studies have shown that 7–10 percent or more of America's school-age children are being prescribed stimulant drugs to control their behavior, and the actual figures may be higher. The percentage of boys being drugged is disproportionately large and probably reaches or exceeds 15–20 percent. One recent survey of two Virginia school districts found that 20 percent of

> fifth grade boys were being administered stimulant drugs during the hours they were actually in school. . . . As we shall document in this chapter, some drug advocates believe that 8 million of America's children should be taking some kind of psychiatric medication.[21]

Dr. Breggin is certainly not alone is his concern. Dr. Lawrence Diller echoes his alarm at the growing statistics:

> Is America ready to have 10 percent of its children taking Ritalin? Because boys are disproportionately represented in the total population of kids diagnosed with ADD, *this would mean giving the drug to one in six boys between the ages of five and twelve.* This prospect seems not to faze some researchers. In their view, if a medication "works" on a certain condition, then we ought to use it.[22]

Before we simply accept the fact that this many children need to be diagnosed and medicated, shouldn't we be very sure that their behavior is truly abnormal? This whole book has been dedicated to bringing awareness about various learning style strengths. There's no doubt that many of these strengths become limitations in the traditional school classroom. Auditory kids can talk too much; visual kids sometimes daydream at the wrong time; kinesthetic kids get in trouble for not sitting still; analytic kids can be too argumentative, and globals can become easily distracted. There are dozens of other pieces to the learning style puzzle that we haven't even addressed, and every piece can bring another positive dimension to each unique and complex individual child.

It is not my intention here to debate or document both sides of the ADHD medication controversy. I have read extensive research and opinion from those who believe ADHD exists and should be a reason to medicate children, those who believe it does not exist and no medication should be given to children under any circumstances, and everything in between. I have to tell you I am becoming a more dedicated member of the second group every year. The more I understand about learning styles, the more troubled I become when I read the list of symptoms for a formal diagnosis of Attention Deficit Hyperactivity Disorder. For example, here is a list of twenty symptoms for ADHD according to Hallowell and Ratey, authors of the frequently quoted book *Driven to Distraction*:

1. A sense of underachievement, of not meeting one's goals (regardless of how much one has accomplished).
2. Difficulty getting organized.
3. Chronic procrastination or trouble getting started.
4. Many projects going simultaneously; trouble with follow-through.
5. Tendency to say what comes to mind without necessarily considering the timing or appropriateness of the remark.
6. An ongoing search for high stimulation.
7. A tendency to be easily bored.
8. Easy distractibility, trouble focusing attention, tendency to tune out or drift away in the middle of a page or a conversation, often coupled with an ability to focus at times.

9. Often creative, intuitive, highly intelligent.
10. Trouble going through established channels, following proper procedures.
11. Impatient; low tolerance for frustration.
12. Impulsive, either verbally or in action, as in impulsive spending of money, changing plans, enacting new schemes or career plans, and the like.
13. Tendency to worry needlessly, endlessly; tendency to scan the horizon looking for something to worry about, alternating with inattention to or disregard for actual dangers.
14. Sense of impending doom, insecurity, alternating with high risk-taking.
15. Depression, especially when disengaged from a project.
16. Restlessness.
17. Tendency toward addictive behavior.
18. Chronic problems with self-esteem.
19. Inaccurate self-observation.
20. Family history of ADD, manic-depressive illness, depression, substance abuse, or other disorders of impulse control or mood.

I don't know about you, but there are an awful lot of symptoms on the above list that closely resemble aspects of my learning style! I don't mean to make light of what many describe as a serious medical condition, but I believe we have to take a good hard look at the behaviors we are letting many professionals tell us must be accepted as abnormal behavior in our children. ADHD should not be thought of as simply a learning disorder—it is officially termed a psychiatric disease, one whose diagnosis and treatment is entered in your child's permanent medical record. It can affect whether or not your child is accepted into the military and how your son or daughter views his or her ability to succeed. And some of the medications used to treat ADHD can even bring on more serious physical diseases.

We cannot afford to assume that when a child doesn't pay attention in school there's something wrong with his or her brain. Before we lay the blame solely on the students, we need to take a closer look at school itself. The first question you should always ask when a teacher implies your child is demonstrating a lack of attention is this: "What were you asking him to pay attention to?" In most cases, that makes all the difference. Thomas Armstrong, a prominent author and educator in multiple intelligences and special learning needs, says this:

> In spite of a spate of reforms in the 1990s, there seems to be a movement back to an even more bleak classroom landscape. Textbooks (and their accompanying worksheets) structure 75 to 90 percent of all the learning that goes on in our schools. . . . U.S. school children are the most tested students in the world, taking more than 100 million standardized tests annually. . . . Schools are even beginning to get rid of recess, so that they can cram more academic learning into kids in preparation for the high-stakes tests at the tend of the term.[23]

Is it any wonder that so many students struggle to pay attention? This doesn't mean we shouldn't hold our kids accountable or that we should only have them do work they consider interesting and fun. But does teaching them discipline and structure mean insisting everyone must learn and perform in the same way? Even students with the most extreme cases of learning disabilities still possess strengths and talents. Sadly, our traditional school system has a rather narrow definition of what is expected when it comes to being academically smart and behaviorally acceptable. More and more students are finding they do not fit into the traditional classroom, and we need to constantly develop new "pull-out" programs to provide students with special help. But if this many students can't deal with the traditional classroom, why aren't we changing the traditional classroom? We keep medicating more and more children so they can perform well in school, and yet we already know that the rest of our lives bear little resemblance to what we had to do in school.

Many bright, capable, intuitive kids are being given labels in school that only serve to make them feel like something is wrong with their brains. But when are we going to start finding out what is wrong with the system? Dr. Mel Levine points out one of the reasons this is so important:

> Labeling is reductionistic. It oversimplifies kids. The practice overlooks their richness, their complexity, their strengths, and their striking originality. Labeling can be dehumanizing; it can consume a person's total identity. It becomes especially scary to me when people can say, "I am ADD." Can you imagine someone proclaiming, "I am bronchial asthma?"[24]

Too often we attempt to keep control in our schools by making sure that only the adults are in charge. We keep the curriculum and the classroom design and the entire system centered around the adults who run it. But the adults aren't the primary customers. The *students* are the customers—and they aren't very satisfied. They don't get much input and they don't get a lot of respect. When they try to let us know what they need, we often insist they should just do what we say for their own good. As adults, we don't have the final word. No matter how carefully we plan or how competently we execute reforms for education, we cannot *force* students to do what we say or to be what we want them to be. In the end, they always have a choice. If we truly want them to make the *right* choices, we have to start with what the *customers* need, not what we need. Just because we've gotten very good at making one or two particular styles of shoes doesn't mean everyone must wear them.

The Homeschool Advantage

Many parents decided to homeschool because they saw their son or daughter headed for trouble in the traditional classroom. When a parent sees their bright, creative, restless, spirited, nonconforming child being daily assaulted by incomplete worksheets, teacher reprimands, low test scores, and failing grades, they want to do whatever they can to make sure that child survives without losing all self-esteem or motivation to learn. But homeschooling isn't for everyone. I remember speaking at a large state homeschool convention a couple of years ago. I was in the ladies' rest room when I overheard someone talking about me in a conspiratorial tone. "I really like her," she said, "even if she *doesn't* homeschool."

Yikes! I have a great deal of admiration for those who are dedicated to homeschooling their children for the right reasons. It's one of the most exhausting, challenging, frustrating, rewarding jobs you can do next to parenting itself. But occasionally there is someone who seems to think less of those of us who choose a different path. It's important to keep your perspective and appreciate the opportunities you are giving your children to learn in an environment that can be much less demanding than the formal school classroom. Obviously no one has a corner on intelligence or creativity, and it's a real privilege to be able to work with public and private-school teachers as well as homeschool parents, all of whom have made the children they teach their top priority.

STRETCHING THE SHOE

Some Practical and Immediate Adaptations

- Ask yourself: How can I make school less boring without doing something that will get me in trouble? Challenge yourself to find ways to cope with your boredom without complaining to the teacher or other students.
- Reconcile yourself to the fact that at least certain aspects of school will simply be "hoops" that you need to jump through in order to achieve your goals. You don't have to love it, or even stop being frustrated, but just knowing it's temporary can help you keep your eyes on the prize.
- Add your own ideas:

____

____

____

CHANGING THE SHOE

Some Ideal Solutions

- Design the classroom to be truly student-centered—define the outcomes ("What's the point?") and challenge the students to find more effective ways of getting there.
- Get more student input—not necessarily about the content or accountability, but about what motivates them, what frustrates them, and what helps them pay attention and accomplish the goals.
- Add your own ideas:

___

___

___

WHY I DON'T WANT TO BE "SCHOOL MATERIAL"

By Cynthia Ulrich Tobias

I don't aspire to be my best
In a big brick building at an old school desk.
I've never planned to sit perfectly still
And not say a word or express my will.
I strive to be different—to be seen and heard—
But not on worksheets full of numbers and words.
I love to talk, but not in pat phrases;
My logic is sound, but I hate to do mazes.
I long to know more, but reading's no pleasure
If it just yields a score you can judge and measure.
I admire those who master their subjects well,
But I tune out the teachers who can't show what
they tell.
I remember so much of what I see and hear,
Yet the tests I am given sure don't make that clear.
What I imagine in my heart and mind
Can't often be captured on notebook lines.
Before you decide how to redesign school,
Why not ask me about outcomes and rules?
I do want to learn how to be my best,
But I can't change the world if I'm just like the rest.

16 Convincing Teachers to Try These Ideas

When the curriculum was engaging—in this case, involving hands-on, interactive learning activities at the junior high school level—students who weren't graded at all did just as well on a proficiency exam as those who were.

—Alfie Kohn, *The Schools Our Children Deserve*

By now, I hope you are enthusiastic about the idea of changing the way we run our schools and teach our students. I hope you are fired up and ready to arm your children with the information and resources necessary to succeed in school, even if nothing *does* change significantly for a while. But how do you convince your child's teachers to keep an open mind to alternate methods of teaching and accountability? How do you get them to understand how important your child's learning style can be when it comes to paying attention and doing homework?

Before I give you some concrete suggestions for persuading your child's teachers to adjust their approach or helping your child adapt to educational demands, let's look at a few basic truths about teachers overall.

Teachers don't teach for the money or the prestige.

Although you often hear people talk about how easy it must be to be a teacher when you get the summers off, don't believe for a minute that they get more vacations than any other working professional. Most teachers spend a great deal of time and money not only getting their initial teaching degree, but also keeping their certification current and obtaining a required fifth year or advanced degree. Many have spent every summer going to school and working a part-time job to pay the extra expenses.

Teachers care about the students they teach.

By far, the majority of teachers—whether in public or private school—care very much about the children in their classroom. It isn't just that they're concerned about the material that must be taught; they know every student has a story, and his or her personal life has a big impact on success in class. Although it isn't possible to address the concerns and issues of each child, most teachers spend a lot of time and effort trying to find effective ways to reach even the most challenging learners.

Teachers are often overburdened by paperwork.

The average teacher can easily end up almost buried in paperwork during the school year. Not only are there forms and record-keeping documents, but there is a constant stream of papers to be graded. As a high school English teacher who also taught drama, I had a total of around 180 students. I consistently had so many student assignments that I often found myself grading spelling papers at stoplights. I discovered that at a good long red light I could get through almost three spelling tests before the driver behind me honked.

Teachers create "disciples" of their students.

I remember one instructor of a graduate education class telling us we should consider the word *discipline* a form of "disciple." Each teacher sets up his or her classroom discipline based on what is important to the teacher—in essence, seeking to make "disciples" of the students who conform to the requirements and approach used. It's not just a system to gain and keep control of the classroom—a good teacher actually has students who reflect the essence of his or her beliefs and convictions. Certainly food for thought . . .

Teachers must answer to administrators, school boards, parents, and communities.

Most teachers are willing to try new methods, and are open-minded enough to stay flexible with their requirements. However, parents often don't realize what an uphill battle a teacher faces when trying to "buck the system." It isn't that teachers or even their administrators refuse to change—but change is daunting when you think about how entrenched the current methods have become. It's no small challenge when it comes to convincing parents and communities that making education more exciting or learner-friendly won't "dumb it down."

Giving the Teacher Information about Your Child

There will always be teachers who seem to care more about your individual child, but it's not usually because all the other teachers don't. Even teachers who have the luxury of a smaller than average class size struggle with finding the time and resources to address each student's individual learning strengths. Some teachers are bound to be more open to your suggestions than others, but there are several things you can do to increase the likelihood of having your child's teacher understand and appreciate the uniqueness of your child's learning style.

First of all, it helps a teacher tremendously to have as much pertinent information about an individual student as possible. As a parent, you need to do your homework and *know your child*. On page 195 you will find a Learning Styles Profile Summary. This worksheet summarizes the points that we've covered in this book. With your child, fill out this profile, then give a copy to your child's teachers to provide them with a concise, nontechnical picture of your child's learning style strengths and preferences.

Remember, you are not making excuses for any inappropriate behaviors or poor work on the part of your child. You are simply focusing on finding and using your child's strengths to overcome limitations and deal with frustration in the traditional classroom. You are letting the teacher know you have done your homework as a parent—you know your child. When you take or send the profile in, be sure to express appreciation for the teacher's education, experience, time, and efforts. Let the teacher know you are open to suggestions for how your child can do his best in the teacher's classroom. It's almost always a good idea to begin a lot of your sentences with the same four words: "What can I do . . . ?" For example, "Martin has a hard time sitting still in class for very long. What can I do to help him learn to cope with that?" "Sarah really struggles to get her math homework done every night. What can I do to help her?"

This approach assures the teacher you are not simply expecting special exceptions for your child or looking for an excuse for poor performance. But it also lets the teacher know you are paying attention and you are willing to be involved in helping your child be successful. Start the school year out with a short note, perhaps attached to your child's profile sheet. Say something positive and simple like, "We're looking forward to your being Adam's teacher this year. We want to work with you and assist wherever you need us." Then include your contact numbers, including home, work, and cell phone numbers—even your e-mail address. This doesn't mean you have to show up and work in the classroom once a week or even once a month. But you can periodically seek out the teacher and ask, "Is there anything I can do to help make your job easier?"

One of our sons had a teacher in third grade who said something at the first of the year parent orientation that made me feel better for months. She told us she knew there were a lot of busy parents out there who simply couldn't come into the classroom during the week or even chaperone field trips or special events. "But," she said, "I want you to know I value your help just as much when it comes in the form of providing supplies we need or buying refreshments, or helping find ways to furnish the classroom with special features." I visibly brightened. I often felt guilty for not getting into the classroom more, but my travel schedule so often prevents it. I do, however, love to shop, and I was already looking forward to using one of my areas of expertise in a way that actually made Mrs. Blum's life in the classroom happier.

What If Your Child Gets a "Bad" Teacher?

I've been in education for over thirty years and worked with schools and teachers in every part of the country. I know there are critics who insist there are many self-serving, incompetent teachers out there who don't really care about children. I have not found that to be true. By far, the vast majority of the teachers I have worked with over the past decades have been committed to their profession and dedicated to the students they teach. There are, of course, certain teachers who are best suited for specific subjects or grade levels. There are also teachers who naturally get along better with some types of students than others. Every teacher has room for professional and personal improvement, just like the rest of us. But as a parent, you should not be overly concerned about your child getting a teacher who is not competent or professional. Your greater concern should be making sure your child and his or her teacher understand each other as well as possible, and learn to work with each other despite their differences.

There are times, of course, when your child may struggle to get along with a teacher, even one he or she loves overall. Even when you as a parent find yourself disagreeing with a teacher, remain friendly and nonthreatening as you search for ways to help your child work out the differences.

One of our sons, Robert, had a teacher in elementary school he dearly loved. Mrs. N valued his creativity and even tolerated his frequent "verbal contributions." It came as quite a surprise to me, then, when Robert ran into trouble with one of his book reports. Robert had read a substantial book about the Wright brothers, and his assignment was to present the report orally in front of the class. Robert prepared for days, telling any of us who would listen about his book—more details than most of us really wanted to hear! He went to Grandpa and figured out what he could wear on the day of the presentation so he would look like Wilbur Wright. The morning of his report he looked quite dashing, and we were all proud of his hard work. That afternoon, I asked him how his presentation went. He shrugged and mumbled, "Okay, I guess." I was surprised. "What grade did you get?" He replied, "I got a C." I was stunned. "Robert, how is that possible? What did Mrs. N say about why you got a C?" He shrugged again and said he just didn't know.

I don't like to challenge a grade given by a teacher, but this one really had me puzzled. I made an appointment with Mrs. N and carefully approached the subject. "I think maybe we misunderstood what was expected of Robert for his book report. He read the book twice, and knew the material inside and out, and yet he got a C on his book report. We're all just a little unsure why." Mrs. N politely explained that the reason Robert's grade was reduced had to do with his lack of following directions, not his lack of reading the book or preparing his report. It turns out he was supposed to use two or three 3 x 5 cards for notes, but Robert had found a 4 x 6 card in my office. He thought it would be much better to put all the information on one card than to have two or three. There were a couple other instances where Robert had skipped a step or a specific instruction, so Mrs. N said his total points were reduced by his failure to follow directions.

I have to admit, I had to swallow hard not to betray my own frustration at the situation. I wanted to say, "But what's the point of a book report? He *read* that book! He *loved* that book! How could you give him a C?" But we all liked Mrs. N. She was a stickler for details, and obviously this time we grossly underestimated the importance of following every single instruction. Robert and I discussed the fact that we all evidently failed to clarify what the point of the oral book report assignment was. Whether or not we agreed with her point of view, we did not find out from the beginning what the point of the assignment really was, and we would certainly be more aware of that from now on.

During the course of your child's K–12 education, there are bound to be some situations where your child and the teacher are simply not a good match. It's important to pick your battles, and to recognize how much you will actually be able to change with regard to how the teacher runs the classroom. Although it doesn't happen often, you may need to go through the necessary channels to simply change classrooms in order to avoid excessive frustration and conflict between your child and a particular teacher.

Shouldn't All Teachers Understand Learning Styles?

What about good teachers who just need to know more about learning styles? How can you make sure the schools where you live are aware of all the wonderful possibilities for keeping standards of achievement and behavior high while still honoring individual learning strengths? I hope you're enthusiastic about the concepts and ideas presented in this book. I hope you're eager to share your enthusiasm with other parents and educators. I also hope you're prepared to encounter some opposition to the whole idea of making our schools more learner-friendly. It's not that teachers don't want their students to become better learners—it's usually a matter of being reluctant to take on yet another program with even more work. In my experience, there are a few key points that need to be addressed when you approach educators with an idea as revolutionary as "What's the point?" learner-centered schools.

1. Always start from the point of accountability. Before you start suggesting ways to help students achieve success in school, make sure the school has agreed with you regarding how they define the goals in the first place. Once you have gotten agreement on what the accountability is, you can ask: "What if I could prove we could achieve that goal a different way?"
2. Reinforce the positive aspects of what teachers are already doing. Give everyone some credit. Many teachers are already tuned in to individual learning styles; you're validating and encouraging their convictions.
3. Be prepared to provide concrete, practical examples of how changing the shoe instead of the foot can make a dramatic difference in students' success.

Tips for approaching the analytic,
step-by-step, no-nonsense style of teacher:

- You'll need to establish the credibility of the research.

- Make any presentations as organized as possible—no ramblings.
- Cite specific examples of success.
- Emphasize results—provide data, if possible.
- Provide a variety of resources.
- Start by valuing each individual's current teaching style; do not press to "convert."
- Keep emphasizing that outcomes will not be sacrificed by varying methods (accountability is intact).
- Point out how this approach will actually help learners become responsible for their own learning by discovering learning style strengths.

Tips for approaching the global, intuitive, capture-the-vision style of teacher:

- Use humor to illustrate your points whenever possible.
- Emphasize the contribution the focus on individual learning styles can make to student self-esteem.
- Recognize the importance of outcomes that are more difficult to measure (attitude, etc.).
- Provide opportunities for group support.
- Encourage teachers to relate learning style concepts to their personal experiences.
- Value flexibility and diverse teaching strategies.
- Offer to help provide concrete and practical support for teachers who want to change their classrooms.
- Focus on how this can change the world of education and the future of the world in very significant ways.

Don't give up! Change may come slowly, but it will be parents and teachers like you who will bring about an effective educational system that values individual differences while providing academic excellence. It's an enormous job, but *somebody's* got to do it!

The Homeschool Advantage

Some homeschool children have never entered a public or private school; others have experienced both the traditional classroom and the homeschool surroundings. As both a parent and a teacher, it's easy to periodically lose your perspective when it comes to how flexible or creative you are being when it comes to educating your child. Try role playing a parent-teacher conference, with your child playing the role of the teacher. You be the parent, and let your child tell you how he or she is doing in class. As the parent, try making two or three suggestions for making your child more successful and see what the "teacher" says. Chances are, both of you will leave the conference with some very interesting ideas!

STRETCHING THE SHOE

Some Practical and Immediate Adaptations

- Create a brief learning style profile of your child at the beginning of each school year, and give a summary to each of his or her teachers.
- Constantly look for ways you can help your child's teacher provide a more comfortable classroom setting or alternatives that he or she would like to try with the students.

- Add your own ideas:

___

___

___

CHANGING THE SHOE

Some Ideal Solutions

- Every undergraduate teacher education program would include course work in learning styles, including practical classroom experience applying the concepts.
- Each teacher would have the opportunity to become part of a group of volunteers on the faculty who meet regularly and support each other by exchanging ideas and insights that motivate and communicate with even the most reluctant learners.
- Add your own ideas:

___

___

___

17 What About Educational Reform?

I would like to see schools change in response to what we now know about the legitimate differences in learning that abound among students at every grade level in every community. . . . To build a mind requires that you understand it.

—Mel Levine, M.D., *A Mind at a Time*

There's no shortage of books and articles about education reform, so the challenge I'm about to issue you should be relatively easy to try. Here it is: Take a yellow highlighter and read one of the articles you find about ideas for reforming education. Throughout the article, every time you see the word *student* or *child* or *learner,* highlight it. Unfortunately, you probably won't use much yellow ink.

Most work that has been done in the name of educational reform has very little to do with students—it's more about structure, measurements, evaluation, assessment, and reorganization. The authors are scholars and researchers and politicians who often know much more about systems than students. For decades we've heard about education being a priority, about the search for more effective ways we can compete with the rest of the world in math and science, about how we can prepare today's students for tomorrow's world. But the reality is, there's been very little change in the fundamental way we treat our children during some of the most important hours they'll spend in their youth.

I am certainly not an expert when it comes to engineering systems or organizing and restructuring, and I don't even pretend to know how to work out all the details involved in revitalizing education. But I do know there are key areas that must be addressed before we can even start to see true improvements in the way our children learn. In some ways, it seems a very daunting task—but we have to start somewhere. Every parent, every teacher, every community member can begin to make a difference when we all agree to put the students first. Let's start by taking a quick look at the key players.

Administrators

Most teachers will tell you that very little can be accomplished when it comes to changing classroom design or teaching methods if there's not support from school and district administrators. If you don't have the administration behind you, you'll wear yourself out trying to implement change, no matter how good the idea seems at the time. On the other hand, if you have administrators and school board members working on your team, you may be amazed at how much you can accomplish. Shirley Griggs and Rita Dunn, in their book *Learning Styles: A Quiet Revolution,* cite several examples of schools and districts who experimented successfully with learning styles in the classroom. At first, they admit, most administrators were skeptical about the changes, thinking it would not only cost more in terms of financial commitment, but also in terms of time and effort trying to get teachers and parents on board. All the schools quoted in Griggs and Dunn's studies were surprised to find out that the obstacles were not nearly as daunting as they thought. One school in rural Texas had great success with students, but the principal was most pleased to find out what effect it had on the whole staff:

> Harp [principal] has so thoroughly embraced learning styles that he has changed his administrative style, saying the model has helped him better understand situations and made him more confident in handling faculty problems and assignments. He perceives problems more as a conflict between styles than a conflict of personalities.[25]

Before you even decide to approach an administrator with a learning styles plan, be sure you practice starting at the end. In other words, begin by coming to agreement on what your outcomes will be—what's the point? When you and your administrator can both agree on the result, you are then in a position to propose alternative ways to achieve it. Bottom-line accountability is never compromised.

The Teachers

As I stated earlier in the book, I believe most teachers care not only about what they're teaching, but also about the students receiving the information. Teachers have never had a broader job description than they do now, and it's not hard to understand why they may feel a little overburdened at the thought of adding yet another duty to their already full schedules. Dr. Diller, in his book *Running on Ritalin,* made an interesting observation from his perspective as a physician being asked to medicate so many students who aren't paying attention:

> This anger that many teachers are feeling these days is understandable. They are asked to share responsibility for the performance and behavior of children from all kinds of backgrounds, with all kinds of problems, and to make adaptations that they feel are difficult or impossible "for the sake of the child." Like the family in which both parents must work to make ends meet, teachers and school systems under pressure find that giving Ritalin to the symptomatic child can help ease the strain. One cannot medicate a school system, however, and it is the child who gets the drug.[26]

The key for teachers, it seems to me, lies primarily in the training they get before they get their original teaching degree. There are many undergraduate courses in teacher training that are hopelessly outdated, and yet most colleges and universities include few, if any, courses on learning styles. There is a strict adherence to the standard textbook courses used through generations of education, and it almost seems irreverent to suggest that teachers learn to teach to all kinds of learners—it seems like we've gone soft, tried to become "entertainers." But William Glasser insists a little entertainment might not be such a bad thing:

> As hard as it may be to accept, we have to sell what we believe is worth learning to those we teach, who may be quite skeptical. A reputable salesman does not try to force you to buy a product: He makes it clear why it is to your advantage to buy what he sells. I don't see why educators consider it beneath their professional dignity to do the same. . . . Almost all we teach is needed, and most students have some idea that this is so. But like many of us who may want something, they still enjoy a

little sell. . . . When people try to force us, even if we think it may be for our own good, we tend to rebel.[27]

Not every teacher has to become an entertainer, but wouldn't it be a breath of fresh air if some of them lightened up a little?

The Parents

Parents have much more power in the public school system than most of them ever dream. For many parents, the world of education is distant and complicated, and it almost seems like educators *want* to keep it a bit of a mystery. There's all that terminology—IEPs and FTEs and bell curves and norms and t-scores. It can be a little intimidating for those who never really liked all that classroom stuff anyway. But it's never been more important for parents to be involved with their children's education. The most important homework should be done not by the student, but the parent. The assignment? *Know your child!*

You can identify your child's learning strengths without any educational training at all. It doesn't take an extraordinary amount of time or expertise—just an interest in knowing how your child learns. For younger children, you can learn a lot by observation. When they are playing the best, where are they? What time of day is it? Who's with them? What seems to keep them happy? For older children, you can ask questions: "What do you need to learn best?" "Where do you like to study?" "What could the teacher do that would make learning easier for you?" You'll find many of these questions in the Learning Styles Profile Summary on page 195. You may also download them from our web site, applest.com.

Parents who become involved with their child's school can make the biggest difference by banding together and forming a support group. Remember to stay very positive—you're not out to change the school through criticism, but through your contribution of positive suggestions, backed up by raising the necessary financial support when it's appropriate. If it's important to you as parents, it won't take long for it to be important to your child's school.

The Community

Today's students are tomorrow's business leaders—a common theme among the chamber of commerce and service organization crowds. The community certainly has a vested interest in making sure the students graduating from their schools are prepared to become productive members of the business world. Dr. Mel Levine is only one of several prominent authors and leaders who are calling for increased community involvement by students while they're still in school:

> Community service in one form or another should be a part of an educational plan. Volunteer work in a hospital, teaching, tutoring, or coaching younger children, and rehabilitating poverty sites are common outlets for kids' basic but often hidden drive to be helpful to others.[28]

Even young children enjoy sharing what they learn with the community. Art exhibits, science fairs, and speech contests are already common methods, but we can get the community even more involved. I did some teacher training in southern California at an elementary school that incorporated an innovative and very successful program.

On Tuesday afternoons, all children grades one through six had the option of attending classes taught by members of the community. The choices included guitar lessons, conversational Spanish, pottery, and other interesting offerings. Each quarter, the children got a new menu of choices, and several new community members got a brief but very rewarding opportunity to get to know their future leaders.

Where Do We Start?

When it comes to educational reform, it's obvious that no one program will ever be able to provide the right answer for everyone. But before we invest in any efforts to reform our schools, we need to make sure we've covered the basics. I'm not talking about reading, writing, and arithmetic; I'm talking about getting a handle on basic learning-styles knowledge and teaching both the teachers and the students how to become more effective learners. Change may come slowly, but it *is* possible to bring about an effective educational system that values individual differences while providing academic excellence. It's an enormous job, but *somebody's* got to do it!

The Homeschool Advantage

One nice thing about homeschooling your children is that your PTA meetings can be short, sweet, and to the point! The whole homeschool movement has already done a great deal to bring attention to the need to improve our educational system. The best thing homeschool parents can do is to continue to demonstrate how effective education can be when it is tailored to the student being taught. Homeschool parents can easily help lead the charge as we develop the most productive and accountable system of teaching and learning while still preserving a child's delight during the process of discovery.

STRETCHING THE SHOE

Some Practical and Immediate Adaptations

- Include the community in as many positive ways as possible, including offering elective classes.
- Challenge the students to find ways to put what they learn into action in the community.
- Add your own ideas:

____

____

____

CHANGING THE SHOE

Some Ideal Solutions

- We need schools where educators, parents, and community all work together, supporting the "What's the point?" approach and accountability.
- Our schools need to be truly centered around the students, not the teachers and administrators.
- Add your own ideas:

____

____

____

18 Choosing the Right School for Your Child

It would be extremely difficult to come up with an exact definition of quality education that would apply to all situations. Even without being able to define it, however, we can almost always recognize quality when we see it. Ask any school administrator to take you through the school and show you some high-quality work in any subject area, and I am certain that you will agree that what you are shown is quality. What is similar about all this work is that none of it could be graded or evaluated by machines—quality never can.

—William Glasser, *The Quality School*

You know every child is unique. You know how important it is that your children have a successful school experience. But how do you know what school will be best for each child? Are all public schools in trouble? Is private school worth the expense? Should you even consider homeschooling your child? What about Montessori, the new charter schools, the classical education, or alternative options?

There is no simple answer to these questions. There is no one school or school system that will work best for all children. Sometimes the public school just down the street from you ends up being the very best situation for your child. Sometimes that private Christian school turns out to be the best investment you ever made, well worth the sacrifice. You may discover that the process of homeschooling your children becomes the most promising alternative for creating success for the whole family.

Before you can make a good choice about the most appropriate school, you will need to have a very good handle on your child's learning strengths. Fill out the Learning Styles Profile Summary on page 195 and discuss it with your child. Think about what causes your child stress, and what makes him or her most comfortable. The most important thing you can do when deciding which school will work best for your child is to find the best fit possible. There may be many other issues that will also influence your decision—financial, geographic, and so on—but you can at least do some fundamental groundwork that can help you identify which type of schooling may best suit your child. Let's look at a few fundamental questions you should have answered before you make a final decision.

Important Questions for Any Kind of Educational Option

1. What kind of ongoing training do the teachers receive? How much training do the teachers get each year?

It's important that teachers have frequent opportunities to enhance their skills and increase their knowledge of both content area and instructional methods. Although most school districts have some excellent local resources, teachers and administrators also need to learn from outside experts and stay up to date on issues through contact with national and international professionals. It would be helpful to know what kind of training is typically offered to the teachers at your child's school, and how much of it is actually required.

2. What kind of educational background do the teachers have (i.e., bachelor's degree, master's degree, local certification)?

In most public schools, teachers must have at least a bachelor's degree from an accredited college or university in order to be certified by the State Department of Education. In many private Christian schools, some of the teachers may still be allowed to teach while they are in the process of getting their four-year degree. Of course, a degree doesn't guarantee that a person is a better teacher. You may discover there are teachers at a particular school who are being asked to teach classes outside their area of expertise. You may also find that a particular school does not require their teachers to keep their credentials current. When you ask about this particular area, always assume the best. Don't appear to be critiquing an individual teacher's educational experience; you are just looking for general information about what is required in order to teach in this particular school or district.

3. What type of student behaviors or attitudes are expected in this school? What type of behaviors and attitudes are particularly unwelcome?

Certain student behaviors and attitudes can usually be expected consistently, regardless of the type of school you are considering—respect for the teacher and each other, common courtesy, and compliance with the rules and regulations of the school. Beyond this, however, you may also be surprised to discover there are some distinct differences between individual types of schools. For example, many charter schools and college prep schools expect much more independent thinking and personal responsibility, beginning at a very young age. Some inner-city public schools may have to insist on more rigid conformity to specific rules and patterns of behavior due to safety or cultural concerns.

Try to determine up front what behaviors and attitudes will be welcome and which ones will be quickly discouraged or swiftly punished. This can be a critical element in finding out how well suited your child may be to the situation.

4. What kind of parental involvement is expected?

You should get a good idea of how much parental involvement is welcome or expected at a particular school. In the case of some cooperative schools, parents are actually required to share classroom and extracurricular responsibilities, and must also agree to mandatory attendance at regularly scheduled parent meetings. Other schools may be much more informal in their approach to parent-teacher relationships. Find out how the school feels about your dropping in occasionally to observe your child's classroom. Ask about communication between your child's teacher and you—will there be regular written updates? How will you know what is expected of you as a parent, and what kind of support should you be giving your child during the school year?

5. How will we know if our child is successful in school?

This can be very revealing when you are trying to figure out how good a match the school situation will be for your particular child. Overall, how does this school measure student success? Are grades a primary factor? How important are standardized test scores? Would a student be considered less successful if he or she excelled on tests but didn't keep up with daily homework assignments? You may find that the best way to approach this subject is to simply ask the school representative to give you the top three ways the school measures a student's success.

6. What are some of the most obvious advantages of attending this school?

If a school has invested a lot of time and effort into making their programs and environment distinctive, it will be easy for a representative to quickly list at least three top reasons their school would be a good choice for your child. You may be surprised to discover how many different answers you'll get from one school to another.

7. For private schools: What are the most important differences between this school and the public schools?

It is completely reasonable for you to ask for specific reasons a private school is worth the considerable financial investment it will take to send your child there. Don't make money the only issue—find out why this particular school believes it is worth whatever it takes to send your child there. Ask for some examples of how this school will benefit your child in the future, and why the extra investment of time and money will be worth it.

8. What kind of student seems to do best in this school?

Each school seems to have its own personality, and it can be important to find out which kind of student seems to excel overall. For example, many private schools place a high emphasis on college preparation. A student who is serious about going on to higher education will usually be most comfortable with what the programs and curriculum require. Other schools may provide more opportunities for vocational education. Many cities offer schools that emphasize areas of specialty, such as drama and the fine arts, science and engineering, and so on. Find out if there is an overall priority on a particular subject area or career focus. You may also want to ask what kind of student tends to struggle most with the school's programs and requirements.

9. What tends to get students in trouble most often? What will happen if our child does not follow the rules?

It's best to know going in what a particular school considers the most troubling discipline problems. There may be a pattern of behavior that is especially unwelcome or some unique circumstances that pose a challenge for certain kinds of students. Ask what kind of situations happen most often, and what the consequences usually are. It's important to know how the school will handle unacceptable behaviors, and how you will be informed if your child is involved.

10. What if our child begins to struggle with the requirements?

It's important to know what kind of help your child can expect to get if he or she gets behind or begins to struggle with particular subjects. Does the school have any specialists or counselors who will be available to help your child find ways to improve? Are there tutors or mentors who are willing to give your child some individual attention? What kind of special programs are in place that can help students who may have difficulty fitting into a traditional classroom? What if your child is actually ahead of the class and seems bored or unchallenged? Although you don't want to appear to be looking for excuses for your child, you do want to be prepared in case he or she needs additional help during the school year.

Should You Homeschool Your Children?

You do not have to be a certified teacher in order to homeschool your children. Each state, however, has different requirements and regulations about homeschool education. You should contact your state's homeschool association and find out as much as you can about what is required.

Not everyone is meant to be a homeschool parent; not every child thrives in a homeschool environment. It's a tough job, and it takes a lot of time and energy to be a full-time teacher over and above being a full-time parent. There can be some wonderful benefits to homeschooling, however, and no one should know what your child needs better than you do. There are thousands of success stories, and so many children have been able to learn better at home than they ever did in a traditional classroom. It's not a decision to be made lightly—if you are considering the homeschool option, be sure you talk to seasoned homeschool parents before you make your final decision.

The Right School for Everyone

In the end, of course, there's only one basic question that must be answered in order to know if you have chosen the right school for each child—does it work? No one type of school will be a perfect match, but the more you know about your child and the more you can discover about the school, the better your chances are of helping each of your children succeed.

Appendix

Learning Styles Profile Summary

Before you can make decisions about specific "shoes" that may fit your child, let's measure the "feet." The following profile summary can provide an informal way to identify the natural learning style strengths we have discussed so far. Remember, these are not boxes or categories—they are more like puzzle pieces. Everyone has every piece—but the pieces are not usually equal in size. Finding out the size of your learning style puzzle pieces can give you invaluable insight into why the foot you bring to school may not fit the shoe offered by the educational system. If you have very young children, you'll want to fill out the summary for them, using your knowledge and observation of their preferences and behaviors. If your children can read, encourage them to fill out the profiles themselves, and then discuss the results with them.

I. How Do You Concentrate? (Environmental Preferences)

Place a mark on the continuum above the description that best fits.

Time of Day

I am usually at my best for thinking and making important decisions:

____

Early morning | Mid-morning | Early afternoon | Mid afternoon | Late afternoon | Early evening | Late evening | Late night

Intake

When I'm studying or concentrating, it helps me to have something to eat or drink

____

It definitely helps | It doesn't really matter | It definitely distracts me

Light

When I'm studying or working,
I work best with this kind of light:

Very bright	Moderately bright	It doesn't really matter	Moderately dim	Very dim

Design

I usually study best when I am in this kind of setting:

Formal, desk or table and chair	It doesn't really matter	Informal—floor, sofa, bed, etc.

Temperature

I have a very hard time concentrating
if the room temperature is too extreme

It's too hot	It doesn't really matter	It's too cold

II. How Do You Remember? (Modalities)

Auditory

When I need to remember something,
I usually need to hear myself talk, discuss with others,
or make a "thinking noise"

Definitely Sometimes Never

Visual

When I need to remember something,
I usually get a picture in my mind, draw,
doodle, or write things down

Definitely Sometimes Never

Kinesthetic

When I need to remember something,
I usually need to move around, take short breaks,
and take some kind of action

Definitely Sometimes Never

III. How Do You Interact with Information?

When it comes to learning and working with information, I tend to be more

Analytic	Both	Global
Focus on specific facts		Focus on main idea
Break information down piece-by-piece		Look at big picture first
Organize in a neat, orderly manner		Organize so I can find things
Work independently		Work together as a group
Prefer step-by-step instructions		Give me the overall idea

Need predictability and preparation	Prefer spontaneity; work by inspiration

What do you think is most important that other people know about your learning style in order to understand you better?

NOTES

1. Peter R. Breggin, M.D., *Talking Back to Ritalin: What Doctors Aren't Telling You about Stimulants and ADHD* (Cambridge, Mass.: Perseus, 2001).
2. Shirley Griggs and Rita Dunn, *Learning Styles: A Quiet Revolution in American Secondary Schools* (Reston, Va.: Learning Styles Network, 1988), 20.
3. Ibid.
4. Ibid.
5. Ibid., 12.
6. Walter Barbe, *Growing Up Learning* (Washington, D.C.: Acropolis, 1985), 68.
7. Ibid., 70.
8. Ibid., 90.
9. Peter R. Breggin, M.D., *Talking Back to Ritalin: What Doctors Aren't Telling You about Stimulants and ADHD* (Cambridge, Mass.: Perseus, 2001), 184.
10. Ibid., 184.
11. Walter Barbe, *Growing Up Learning* (Washington, D.C.: Acropolis, 1985), 59.
12. Dr. James Dobson, *Dr. Dobson's Monthly Newsletter*, November 1997, www.family.org/docstudy/newsletters/a0000072.html.
13. William Glasser, *The Quality School: Managing Students without Coercion* (New York: HarperCollins, 1998), 120.
14. Mel Levine, M.D., *A Mind at a Time* (New York: Simon & Schuster, 2002), 314.
15. Ibid., 326.
16. Walter Barbe, *Growing Up Learning* (Washington, D.C.: Acropolis, 1985), 178.
17. Thomas Armstrong, *In Their Own Way* (New York: Penguin Putnam, 2000), 15.
18. Ibid.
19. Not his real name.

20. Lucy Jo Palladino, *The Edison Trait* (New York: Times Books, 1997), xiv.
21. Peter R. Breggin, M.D., *Talking Back to Ritalin: What Doctors Aren't Telling You about Stimulants and ADHD* (Cambridge, Mass.: Perseus, 2001), 3.
22. Lawrence H. Diller, *Running on Ritalin: A Physician Reflects on Children, Society, and Performance in a Pill* (New York: Bantam, 1998), 37.
23. Thomas Armstrong, *In Their Own Way* (New York: Penguin Putnam, 2000), 5.
24. Mel Levine, M.D., *A Mind at a Time* (New York: Simon & Schuster, 2002), 328.
25. Shirley Griggs and Rita Dunn, *Learning Styles: Quiet Revolution in American Secondary Schools* (Reston, Va.: Learning Styles Network, 1988), 10.
26. Lawrence H. Diller, *Running on Ritalin: A Physician Reflects on Children, Society, and Performance in a Pill* (New York: Bantam, 1998), 159.
27. William Glasser, *The Quality School: Managing Students without Coercion* (New York: HarperCollins, 1998), 123.
28. Mel Levine, M.D., *A Mind at a Time* (New York: Simon & Schuster, 2002), 326.

LEARNING STYLES: AN ANNOTATED BIBLIOGRAPHY FOR EDUCATORS

Armstrong, Thomas. *Awakening Your Child's Natural Genius: Enhancing Curiosity, Creativity, and Learning Ability.* New York: G.P. Putnam's Sons, 1991. Armstrong's premise is that every child has the seeds of brilliance—they just need the right opportunities to bloom. This book is filled with practical strategies for making it happen.

________________. *In Their Own Way: Discovering and Encouraging Your Child's MultipleIntelligences.* New York: Penguin Putnam, 2000. A practical, encouraging book for parents and teachers, this will provide you with insights and strategies for helping children understand how they are smart and appreciate how they are designed.

________________. *The Myth of the A.D.D. Child: 50 Ways to Improve Your Child's Behavior and Attention Span without Drugs, Labels, or Coercion.* New York: Dutton, 1995. A former special education teacher, Dr. Armstrong provides fifty practical, positive ways to help that child who has been labeled ADD. His heartfelt and well-researched position is that ADD does not exist; that the children who experience behavior and attention problems are healthy human beings with a different style of thinking and learning.

________________. *7 Kinds of Smart: Identifying and Developing Your Multiple Intelligences.* New York: Penguin Putnam, 1999. A revised and updated volume of Armstrong's first edition—this one includes a practical and informative explanation of Gardner's two newest intelligences: Naturalist and Existential.

Barbe, Walter B. *Growing Up Learning.* Washington, D.C.: Acropolis, 1985. Although this book is currently out of print, you'll find your trip to the library to read it will be well worth your while! The former editor of *Highlights* magazine shares a wealth of information about auditory, visual, and kinesthetic modalities. You'll find age-appropriate checklists, and dozens of suggestions for helping your child learn in many different ways.

Breggin, Peter R. *Talking Back to Ritalin: What Doctors Aren't Telling You about Stimulants for Children.* Cambridge, Mass.: Perseus, 2001. According to Dr. Breggin, most doctors can't tell you the truth about drugs for treating your children's behavior, because even doctors haven't been told the truth about the drugs they prescribe. In this compelling book, Dr. Breggin shows why our children need education, not medication.

Breggin, Peter R., and Ginger Ross Breggin. *The War against Children: How the Drugs, Programs, and Theories of the Psychiatric Establishment Are Threatening America's Children with a Medical "Cure" for Violence.* New York: St. Martin's, 1994. Dr. Breggin is a psychiatrist who has taken a stand against the use of medication for social control of children and their behaviors. He and his wife have written this compelling book, providing a host of alternative measures for fulfilling the genuine and often inconvenient needs of children.

Chess, Stella, and Alexander Thomas. *Know Your Child: An Authoritative Guide for Today's Parents.* New York: Basic, 1987. A credible and enlightening look at research that demonstrates with compelling results how a child's temperament and individual differences determine a "goodness of fit" with their world.

Cline, Foster, and Jim Fay. *Parenting with Love and Logic: Teaching Children Responsibility.* Colorado Springs, Colo.: Piñon, 1990. If you want to raise kids who are self-confident, motivated, and ready for the real world, take advantage of this win-win approach to parenting. The information in this book can not only revolutionize your relationships with your children, but can also put the fun back into parenting!

Diller, Lawrence H., M.D. *Running on Ritalin: A Physician Reflects on Children, Society, and Performance in a Pill.* New York: Bantam, 1998. As a pediatrician and family therapist, Dr. Diller presents a compelling, credible, common sense look at the controversial issue of medication and ADHD diagnoses in children.

Fay, Jim, and David Funk. *Teaching with Love and Logic: Taking Control of the Classroom.* Golden, Colo.: Love and Logic Press, 1995. This book will give you practical solutions to the day-to-day frustrations and challenges common in today's classroom. Following these tried-and-true techniques can reduce the time and energy you spend maintaining discipline in the classroom, and let you put some fun back into teaching.

Glasser, William, M.D. *The Quality School: Managing Students without Coercion.* New York: HarperCollins, 1998. Dr. Glasser's often controversial concept of a quality school where there is no failure because all students are doing competent work and are doing quality work.

Glenn, H. Stephen, Ph.D., and Michael L. Brock, M.A. *7 Strategies for Developing Capable Students.* Rocklin, Calif.: Prima, 1998. Common-sense approach to helping our children become capable, significant young people who know how to think and make good decisions. The authors provide many encouraging words and practical tools for developing responsibility, self-discipline, and communication skills in children.

Keirsey, David, and Marilyn Bates. *Please Understand Me: Character and Temperament Types.* Del Mar, Calif.: Prometheus, Nemesis, 1978. This book provides a fascinating look at personality type and temperament. You'll discover how your temperament affects your success in relationships, careers, and life in general.

Kohn, Alfie. *The Schools Our Children Deserve: Moving beyond Traditional Classrooms and "Tougher Standards."* New York: Houghton Mifflin, 1999. An ambitious and provocative vision of how our schools should be rethinking our most basic assumptions about schooling.

Levine, Mel, M.D. *A Mind at a Time.* New York: Simon and Schuster, 2002. One of the best-known pediatricians and education experts in America today brings a fresh, practical perspective backed with years of research and practice to the concept of learning differences.

Schultz, Thom, and Joani Schultz. *The Dirt on Learning: Groundbreaking Tools to Grow Faith in Your Church.* Loveland, Colo.: Group, 1999. Fresh, practical insights and strategies that can revolutionize how you teach and lead children, youth, and adults.

Tobias, Cynthia Ulrich. *Do You Know What I Like about You? Jumpstarting Virtues and Values in Your Children.* Ann Arbor, Mich.: Vine, 1997. A celebration of the ways in which we as adults deal with children in our lives. This collection of narrative, photographs, and poetry will surely touch and inspire hearts and minds.

______________. *Every Child Can Succeed: Making the Most of Your Child's Learning Style.* Colorado Springs, Colo.: Focus on the Family, 1995. This book is filled with practical ideas for applying learning styles to motivation, discipline, and much more.

______________. *The Way They Learn: How to Discover and Teach to Your Child's Strengths.* Colorado Springs, Colo.: Focus on the Family, 1994. An international best-seller, this entertaining and practical book introduces the basics of learning styles for parents or teachers who want to help their children succeed.

______________. *The Way We Work: A Practical Approach for Dealing with People on the Job.* Colorado Springs, Colo.: Focus on the Family, 1995. An enlightening and easy-to-read resource for developing efficient communication with those with whom you work. This is a powerful plan for transforming your on-the-job relationships!

EDUCATIONAL PHILOSOPHY STATEMENT

AppLe St. (Applied Learning Styles)

Cynthia Ulrich Tobias, M.Ed., founder and CEO

We believe each person is created with unique and special strengths, abilities, and perspectives.
Therefore, we are committed to the following:

- Identifying and building on strengths to produce positive results rather than focusing on limitations;
- Appreciating the worth and value of every style, recognizing there is no best or smartest style;
- Honoring individual learning style differences without compromising academic excellence or lowering standards of behavior;
- Maintaining discipline through love and bottom-line accountability within the framework of each person's design; and
- Unlocking the potential for success in both children and adults by teaching them *The Way They Learn*.

Cynthia Ulrich Tobias
AppLe St. LLC, PO Box 1450, Sumner, WA 98390.
(253) 862-6200; Fax (253) 891-8611; e-mail: applest@aol.com
web sites: applest.com; cantmakeme.com; thestrongwilledwoman.com

Redefining the Strong-Willed Woman

How to Effectively Use Your Strong Will for God

Cynthia Ulrich Tobias

Many strong-willed women have secretly wondered if there was something wrong with them, if perhaps they just weren't trying hard enough to be good conforming Christian women. Cynthia Tobias provides a compelling and practical way for strong-willed women to come together and identify themselves to each other and the world.

In Christian circles, women are often reluctant to come right out and say they are strong willed and proud of it. They have somehow been persuaded that God wouldn't approve of a woman who is so—well, nonconforming. After all, isn't the virtuous woman supposed to be quiet, holy, and subservient? Tobias reminds readers that the single most important thing they will ever do is accept Jesus Christ as their personal savior. But beyond that, God gave each person their unique personality, gifts, learning styles, passions, and desires. He created and designed each person before they were even born.

Whether readers see themselves as strong-willed women or just need to understand the strong-willed women in their lives, *Redefining the Strong-Willed Woman* provides powerful insight and encouragement for all types of women and men.

Hardcover: 0-310-24578-8